FRIENDKEEPING

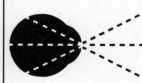

This Large Print Book carries the
Seal of Approval of N.A.V.H.

FRIENDKEEPING

A FIELD GUIDE TO THE PEOPLE YOU LOVE, HATE, AND CAN'T LIVE WITHOUT

JULIE KLAM

THORNDIKE PRESS
A part of Gale, Cengage Learning

GALE
CENGAGE Learning·

Detroit • New York • San Francisco • New Haven, Conn • Waterville, Maine • London

GALE
CENGAGE Learning®

LIBRARY OF CONGRESS CATALOGING-IN-PUBLICATION DATA

Klam, Julie.
   Friendkeeping : a field guide to the people you love, hate, and can't live without / by Julie Klam. — Large Print edition.
     pages cm. — (Thorndike Press large print nonfiction)
   Originally published: New York : Riverhead Books, c2012.
   Includes bibliographical references.
   ISBN-13: 978-1-4104-5646-5 (hardcover)
   ISBN-10: 1-4104-5646-3 (hardcover)
   1. Friendship. 2. Interpersonal relations. I. Title.
   BF575.F66K53 2013
   158.2'5—dc23   2012045641

Published in 2013 by arrangement with Riverhead Books, a member of Penguin Group (USA) Inc.

Printed in the United States of America
1 2 3 4 5 6 7 17 16 15 14 13

FOR VIOLET JEAN LEO,
THE ONLY FRIEND I EVER
REALLY MADE

Dear George:
  Remember <u>no</u> man is a failure who has <u>friends.</u>
  Thanks for the wings!

Love,
Clarence

— *IT'S A WONDERFUL LIFE*

CONTENTS

INTRODUCTION

I'm a middle-aged person who uses the term "BFF" without irony. I am, to put it simply, crazy about friendships. It's even in my astrological chart. I don't really know what it all means, but I'm an Aquarius rising. Apparently, we Aquarius-rising types put the emphasis on friendships first and foremost in our lives. Not only that, but Jupiter is in my eleventh house, and the eleventh is the house of friends. Every psychic and astrologer I've talked to — and believe me when I say I've talked to a lot of them — has told me the same thing: Friends are very, very valuable to me, and they will always matter a great deal in my life. And who am I to argue with the stars?

Years ago, I read an article about a famous actress who annually takes a group of her best friends on a Caribbean vacation. They have a house right on the beach with a cook and a maid. They play board games, listen

11

to music, drink wine, and eat "chocolate chip cookies the size of your head." They give one another beauty treatments, watch movies, and walk on the beach, but mostly they talk and talk and talk. Just the actress and her besties. She said that with her frequent long months of making movies, she didn't get the time to hang out with her friends the way she wanted to, and this was her necessary friendship maintenance. It was a celebration of her friends. Doesn't that sound like heaven? A big cluster of uninterrupted time in paradise with only your friends, and someone else to clean the hair out of the shower drain.

That's always been my "if (when) I hit the lottery" fantasy. Fortunately, the kind of work I do rarely places me on location in Belize for eight months, so I can have smaller celebrations of my friends. Like a relaxing picnic in the park on a summer day or a frantic race against time at a sample sale — whatever it is, we can talk and talk and talk, and maybe have a chocolate chip cookie the size of your nose.

My mother claims I was making playdates from my bassinet in White Plains Hospital. She was always a little puzzled by my über-sociality. She said that in kindergarten I would take the big avocado-colored hall phone and my class list and sit on the floor and call one kid after another. It didn't matter who, it just mattered that someone came over to play. "All you want is a body!" my mother declared. I like to think it was egalitarian of me. I know I was lonely, but I loved having a friend over more than anything. Oh, the joys of playing dolls with another dollophile! My two brothers had each other to play with, and wouldn't include me unless their game required a dead body or a stenographer. So I would have a friend over, a very special friend, one who answered the phone and could get a ride.

As long as I have known her, my mother has put her relationship with her sisters before her friends, and this has informed her viewpoint on my friendships. She didn't get my obsession with friends. Though she had "tennis friends" and "horse friends," and might sometimes grab coffee with another kid's mother, when she really wanted to talk, she'd dial her flesh and blood. I used to think it was weird, like twins who have their own language, but when I got older I realized that I liked hanging out with my mother and her sisters, too. Her youngest sister, Mattie, is actually one of my closest friends. She was even maid of honor at my wedding. But I didn't have that kind of relationship with my brothers when we were kids. Friendships were much more critical to me.

Other than availability, my early friendships were based on a deeply shared belief system: Princesses were excellent to play and draw; Barbies were fun, but forget the shoes; rainbows were good; makeup was to be applied heavily. There were no politics to deal with, except for the one little girl who shocked me by proclaiming that her dad had voted for Nixon.

In the early years, my behavior in friendships tended toward the bossy. I was domineering, yes, but also unusually generous. I'd give away my stuff. It drove my mother crazy. I'd invite someone over, and the kid would leave with my new jewelry set. I just wanted to make my friends happy. I thought that should include a parting gift. My mother recently pointed out that the object of much of my gifting was a little girl whose father owned most of lower Manhattan. I would like to find her now and see if maybe I could get my Raggedy Ann necklace back . . . or maybe a penthouse apartment.

Early elementary school was rather pleasant for me. I believed then that the world was somewhat fair and made sense. Kids were friendly unless you bit them. And then, around fourth grade, Mean Girls entered the forest. Oy, the enormous havoc the years of cliques and lemon parties and slam books wreaked on my friendships. My mother assured me that girls were mean only because they were jealous. This made total sense, except I did poorly in school, had perpetually greasy hair, and would destroy any team's chance of winning a game if I was included. Yet somehow my mother convinced me that these flaxen-haired, swim team–grooving playground idols were threatened by me. This line of thinking of my mother's would pretty much continue through, oh, next Thursday at two p.m.

When I was in college and wondered why no guys were asking me out, my self-appointed sociologist mother explained they were all threatened by my magnificent brains and razorlike wit. It was an excellent and unbiased worldview, which I would sadly discover had not a shred of reality in it.

Somewhat obviously, the meaning and roots of my friendships have changed throughout my life. They have become more profound to me, are based on more depth, though recently I did make a friend because we were both looking for vichyssoise at Zabar's. Childhood friendships were so fraught with obstacles: insecurity, identity issues, peer pressure, fear. Adolescent relationships included all of those things, as well as hormonal surges, acne, and impulse bangs-cutting. By college, I began to have an inkling of who I was and what mattered to me. But when I had stopped giving away my toys, I started giving away too much of myself. I would listen to friends' problems for hours and hours, and when they finally asked me how I was, I'd simply say, "Fine." I wondered why I felt so taxed and ener-vated, and ultimately realized that I wasn't getting out of these friendships what I was putting into them. When my friends finished talking, I just wanted to go home to my Star Wars trilogy and bowl of Golden Grahams.

Turned out, I wasn't very good at recipro-cal friendship. I was a good listener and advice giver, but I couldn't figure out how to properly share and ask for help from my friends. I had a great fear of being a burden, and so bitterness would build, and I became even more closemouthed. I'd do anything to avoid confrontation. I assumed if I was ever anything but agreeable, my friends wouldn't like me anymore. Instead, I got so uncomfortable the friendships failed for that reason.

One Sunday night, after spending a weekend of going to movies and museums and diners by myself, I was sitting on my couch trying to smell the straps of my backpack. I was at the fork in the road, with one arrow pointing toward "Insane Bearded Woman with Pet-Babies in a Carriage" and another toward "Relatively Normal." I had a choice: Get back to making new friends or hole up and write a manifesto. Slowly and carefully, I started meeting people who I felt could reciprocate. I learned that it was gratifying for other people to listen and help their friends, just as it was for me. Now I have a lot of fairly perfect close friends — and even more people I really like but don't get to see enough. To borrow a line from my daughter's kindergarten class, I am the captain of my own friendships.

Of course, there are problems in friendships. Relationships aren't perfect, people aren't machines. Our lives go through myriad changes. One week I may be the perfect friend, sending you a "Just because I care" card, and the next I'm stressed out and forgetting our lunch date. Hopefully, it's somewhere in the middle, or at least a place where we can work with it. I'm amazed at how frequently adult friendships put me right back on the playground, sitting on the splintery side of the seesaw. I have to remind myself that now I possess the tools to thrash out a problem. Also, I have a driver's license.

I feel a little bit like the luckiest (wo)man on the face of the earth to have so many truly wonderful close friends who support me, crack me up, and enrich my life in unique ways. I think my friends are my best quality. Hey, maybe the fact that I've been able to make them and keep them *does* make me something of a friendship expert!

In the coming pages you'll meet them, too. Barbara, whom I met on the first day of fifth grade, when she walked into my class wearing red pants with a white bicycle print. We stayed friends through junior high and high school, broke up for a bit in college, then got right back together and have been here ever since. She's strong and brave and honorable, but she'll beat the crap out of you in any board game you are foolish enough to play with her.

Jancee and I met on a hayride in the nineties, immediately bonding over our discomfort of sitting on straw. She and I have been through a lot together. She is a lot like me, but stronger in all the ways I struggle, so I can always count on her to give me a nudge to do the work. She's screamingly hilarious, and nothing grosses her out.

Patty and I met at our agent's mother's funeral (our agent is also our good friend). When she says something, I often think, Who does she remind me of? and I realize it's me in my head — the things I'd never say out loud but wish I could. She's funny and fast, and she has no food in her refrigerator.

Ann and Laura are close friends, and we cohost a radio show. Ann is old-fashioned, no-nonsense, do-what-has-to-be-done, and even though she's only a couple of years older than I am, she's got the mother vibe; I can always ask her for help with something stupid. Laura and I managed to become pretty close friends before meeting face-to-face. She reminds me a lot of me, and I know there's no awful thought about something that I can't say to her that she won't understand and validate.

As my friendships grow stronger and closer (and older), their meaning continues to deepen, especially as I watch my eight-year-old daughter stepping further into the world of friends, navigating the scary parts and giddy over the first sleep(less)over. And on the other end, I'm seeing my seventy-three-year-old mother beginning to say good-bye to dear old friends.

Lasting friendships are kind of a miracle, but one that can't be neglected. They need nurturing and thought, caring, and even a bit of preparation for the conflicts and challenges that arise. Friendship might be free, but it requires a real, solid investment. And you know, the occasional baked good never hurts.

CHAPTER 1
I'VE GOT A SECRET

I'm a huge believer in being truthful except in the instances of hurting someone's feelings or saving your own ass. (The saving-your-own-ass reason doesn't really apply to this chapter or this book; in fact, pretend I didn't say it.)

I've often felt that the sharing of information between parents is one of the most vital and useful tools of parenting. It's also the quickest way to find out that not only are all of your fears utterly justified, there's also more scary junk that you weren't smart enough to know about and your lack of awareness may have just destroyed your child's chances of getting into any institution that doesn't have bars on the windows.

The summer before Violet started first grade, we were in the playground with her friend Sylvia and Sylvia's mom, Jenny, who was one of my few mom-friends at the time. Jenny and I were talking about the following year and which teachers were supposed to be good.

"I don't really know much about the teachers," Jenny said, "but if Syl gets Jane Doe, I'm going to kill myself."

"Uh-oh, what's her story?" I asked.

Jenny went on to tell me a list of nightmarish (on a first-grade level) stories about Miss Doe. She was strict and kind of scary and possibly a meanie. It wasn't clear exactly what her problem was. What was clear was that I didn't want her, and I just *knew* Violet would get her.

A few days later I got the card in the mail with Violet's teacher assignment. Terry Bass, the friendly scarecrow of teachers, was crossed out, and Jane Doe was written on it. Because that's the kind of luck I had. The gods gave Violet nice pushover Terry Bass, and my luck came in and scribbled her name out and stuck in Satan. I texted Jenny and told her Violet got Jane Doe, and Jenny said, "I'm sure it will be fine." And, "I should never have told you that."

I told her I didn't care. I figured everyone's relationships with teachers are different. One person's favorite is another one's worst nightmare.

The bigger problem was that, although Violet's teacher had told me at the end of kindergarten that each of the kids would have at least one friend in their first-grade class, because of a confluence of clerical errors, Violet had no friend and did not even know anyone in her class. While in my logical mind I knew that it was highly unlikely that any of this would affect her life — "You see, she didn't get into Dartmouth because she had *no friend from kindergarten placed with her in first grade*!" — my emotional self was reeling.

Violet began first grade, and from the start I was scared of Miss Doe. She wasn't one of the laid-back friendly types; she came across as humorless and stern. In the morning, if the kids got to the schoolyard after the class line started moving toward the building, even if they caught up with the line, they'd be marked late. There was zero tolerance, and I had a kid who never met a rule she couldn't work around. Except here things were different. Since Violet was no longer a kindergartner, she was a FIRST GRADER, a certain adherence to laws would be necessary. I tried very hard to get Miss Doe to like me, but she wasn't having any of it. She didn't gab with the parents, she had her eyes on the class. When I told her we were moving to a different apartment the week after school started, she rolled her eyes like I was doing it just to wreck everyone's year.

A few weeks later Violet came home from school and pulled a very nice pen out of her bag.

"Where did you get that?"

"Miss Doe gave it to me."

"Really?" I said.

"Yes, she told me that I was such a good student that I could pick anything I wanted off her desk to have," Violet told me. "I chose between this pen and a plastic iguana."

I was taking in her words, my eyebrows slowly beginning to come down. My kid wasn't a liar, she just wasn't. But this story wasn't making sense. She went on to tell me more details about the things Miss Doe had said about her, how Violet was the most special kid in the class and better than anyone else, and some other interesting questionable details.

"Are you telling me the truth?" I asked my sweet little cherub.

She smiled. "No." Her smile grew bigger. "I just took it."

I thought about pulling her out of school. I'd homeschool her, or get her into the witness protection program. Maybe we could say some other kid, that bad kid, Jeremy, put the pen in her bag, in essence framing her. He would be getting in trouble for something else anyway so what would it hurt?

"Am I going to go to juvie?" Violet asked. She had a friend in school who frequently discussed the things she might do that would get her thrown into juvie.

"Of course not!" I said, doubting myself as I talked. "Tomorrow just stick the pen back on her desk when she isn't looking, okay?" I said casually. "Okay?"

I'm a tad mortified sharing this; it wasn't my finest moment in motherhood.

"I don't think I can do that, Mom," Violet said. "I think you need to talk to Miss Doe."

Me? Why me? I didn't steal the damn pen!

"All right," I said, "give me the pen." I had a sickening feeling like I wanted to throw up, and then, at that moment, my backbone grew three sizes larger.

"I'll talk to Miss Doe tomorrow," I said.

I didn't sleep that night. I thought about mass murderers you'd hear about who tortured animals when they were kids. Was this a sign of some life of crime to come?

I was afraid. The next day I marched us into school and walked up to Miss Doe.

"Excuse me, I need to speak with you," I said, doing my best parental impression.

She turned to me. I knew it was a little rule-breaking of me to just approach her like that; she had said she preferred notes to being approached, but I had to talk to her.

"I'm really sorry," I said, "but VIOLET STOLE YOUR PEN!"

A warm smile came over her face, and she shook her head and said quietly, "It's okay, my daughter did the same thing. It doesn't mean she's a thief." I was shaking with relief, holding back tears. (How idiotic was I? I think that's becoming clear.) Apparently, Violet had been testing Miss Doe in a variety of ways, but she also seemed to want me to have a reason to talk to her. I think it bothered her that I didn't really have a relationship with her teacher. (The teacher, incidentally, ended up being one of the best we ever had.) She wanted to see me interacting with her instead of running away every day. (By the way, I do *not* recommend having a kid who is smarter than you — it can really cause problems.)

After it was over, I was so relieved I started thinking about the whole "Honesty is the best policy" line that I eschewed. I thought, Maybe there's something to it. *Maybe.* You know, was there a place for honesty?

I do truly feel, though, that there isn't

26

enough credit given to the importance of temporary dishonesty. Keeping information to yourself is not the same as lying. For instance, United States presidents should always be honest, but they can't go into a press conference and say, "I'm so excited about the terror cell in Mexico City we just found out about. A bunch of our guys are going down there right now to blow them up." In fact, I frequently think of my own life in terms of military secrets. You know, because the truth is too painfully boring. That's another very good reason not to tell your friends certain things — you don't want to divulge too many mundane details, unless, like the people in my family, they like to hear every single thing you ate the day before.

About twelve years ago, something big happened to me, and I wasn't allowed to tell . . . until it was officially announced. Eventually I would be allowed to tell, but not yet. Get it? I called up Jancee and told her that I needed to talk to her, that I had to tell her something but she couldn't tell anyone.

"Oh, no." She worried.

"It's not bad," I assured her.

"No," she clarified, "I just don't know if I want to know. What if I tell someone by accident?"

"How would you do that?"

"Well, like if I talk in my sleep or something." Jancee and I grew up on seventies TV shows, where many, many secrets were divulged in clear sentences by someone who was fully asleep while another person — the person who would be the *worst one* to find out the secret — was walking by the room at the time with, by some crazy bad TV luck, a *tape recorder.*

"If you talk in your sleep, hopefully Tom [her husband] won't tell anyone."

"What if I fall asleep on the subway and blurt it out?" she said.

I sometimes refer to Jancee as "my best friend Howard Hughes" because she is such a crazy germophobe; she has thighs of steel because she's never, ever sat on a toilet seat (I don't even think in her own house). The idea that she'd be on a subway, relaxed enough to doze off and possibly risk leaning her head back on the place where billions of greasy pates have rested, was about as likely as her licking the handrail.

"Do you want me not to tell you?" I asked.

"No, Jul, what kind of friend am I?" she said. "You need to talk about something and I need to be able to hear it."

I should mention that this conversation

started on the phone on a Tuesday and continued into Thursday, when we had lunch at Saks. We took a slight detour to talk about every secret she had ever heard and kept. And that my secret getting out wasn't going to interfere with National Security. It was more about the stress that the impending secret was putting on her, and I started wondering about the ramifications of the confidences we share with friends. Ultimately, after she scoured for bugs (the recording kind, not the germy kind), I told her. She braced herself, inhaled, and when I said it, she stopped and said, "You told me that already."

That's me. That's her.

My brilliant aunt Mattie once said to me, "If you have a secret and you can't keep it, don't expect anyone else to do a better job than you."

Here's some stuff to remember:

I guarantee that at some point in your life, something you told someone not to tell anyone ever was told to many, many other people with that same instruction.

If there's something you don't want anyone to know: Don't. Tell. Anyone.

If you simply have to tell someone, choose a person who's taken some sort of oath . . . like a Good Humor man.

Think about why you want to share this information. Is it worrisome to you? Would it make sense to bring this to a professional? Is it gossipy and you want to have a little fun?

I pretty much as a rule am not a person with secrets (see: memoirist). But occasionally something interesting happens to me or someone I know and then I am a carrier.

I met one of my closest friends, Patty, at the funeral of our agent's mother. We became fast friends when she showed me that she could imitate the Lord & Taylor script logo. I gave her a pen and in seconds she'd shown me a talent I'd never dreamed of. Her first book had just come out, and mine was due out soon. We were both in a very similar place, and the things we were dealing with, which upon hearing would have bored any regular person into taking their own life, were delicious nuggets to each other. I read her book and loved it, and a friendship was born. The first time we got together I said, "Don't tell anyone this, but —" And she interrupted to tell me what a world-class secret keeper she was. I realized this was true when I found out who her closest friends were — some of the most famous people in the world. And she wasn't blabbing. (The secret I had to tell her was something that wasn't so much a secret as embarrassing, so, you know, don't feel bad that I'm not writing about it here.)

That's what I call a Class 3 secret. This is the secret that you tell a million people not to tell anyone, really because you don't want it published or Facebooked about or someone to bring it up to you at a party surrounded by fifteen strangers. Examples of a Class 3 are: number of rejections you've gotten on something; job you applied for but didn't get; injection of some sort of youthening serum or cosmetic surgery; person you had sex with a long time ago.

There is no Class 2 secret. It's either a Class 3 or a Class 1.

The Class 1 is serious, potentially damaging/hurtful if it were to get out. I don't have to give you examples of those. If you want to know what I mean, tune in to Maury Povich's show, where daily you will find a bunch of examples of people who think there is only one acceptable way to share a Class 1 secret — in front of a national audience.

I love my friend Adam. He and I met in 1986 when I was interning on *Late Night with David Letterman* and he was a writer. I know a lot of funny people and he might just be the funniest, which is saying a lot. He's pretty much my only male friend. You know those women who say, "I'm only friends with guys"? They're usually too "hot-looking" to be friends with women? Well, that ain't me. I like to talk about gross girl things and weird hairs, and sometimes I'll talk for a really long time about whether or not I want to try false eyelashes. Adam, whom I sometimes call Ad or Addy or Unky Ad, is a perfect person to tell a secret to because, as he says, he doesn't know anyone who'd care. He is married, he will tell his wife, Lorrie, and that's understood. But he's not a big blabber; also, he forgets things almost as quickly as I say them. Sometimes I'll remind him that I told him something fifty times already and then he worries about dementia because he's in his late forties and then I remind him he didn't remember stuff when he was in his mid-twenties and we all feel better and no one really cares what I have to say anymore. Another person guaranteed not to talk? My dogs. I love the freedom of telling my dogs a huge secret in full detail. "Beatrice, Larry's sister is having an affair with Ted Turner!" She's like the sphinx. She would never utter a word, and she's always rapt.

You need to know your friends. You know

if someone is good at keeping a secret or not. I know you can think of that one person right now who isn't. It's not their fault; it's like a disease, blabaholism. I truly believe that if you tell someone iffy like that something they aren't supposed to say, and they tell, you deserve what you get. A leopard doesn't change its big-mouth spots. I had a friend a long time ago, a good person who just, as my mother would say, had diarrhea of the mouth. She heard "Don't tell anyone" as "Speed dial your top ten friends and tell them this." The first couple of times it happened, she was genuinely sorry and seemed confused. "Oh, *that* was the thing I wasn't supposed to tell? I thought I wasn't supposed to tell that you told me not to tell," or something equally misunderstood. And I kind of believed her, but I also knew that a tasty bit of gossip was just too much for her to keep.

Friends need to share some secrets with each other. Sometimes private situations can feel unbearably burdensome; knowing you have a confidant who can be sympathetic and discreet makes life's loads infinitely lighter. But you don't need to share all of your secrets and you don't need to hear everything from your friends. Not telling a friend something hurtful or sensitive is not the same as being dishonest. No one really wants to know when their ass looks big.

CHAPTER 2
THROUGH SICK AND THIN

For a long, long time I was very, very lucky. The only people I knew who died were quite old and somewhat removed from me. My family and friends were healthy; I didn't worry about bad things happening to the people I cared about because they just didn't.

Jancee and I used to talk about it. I was at lunch with her one day and I said, "You know, when I die —" And she said, "*If* — if you die." And we both laughed, but on some level it actually sounded right. I mean, I wasn't going to die. She wasn't going to die. Why would we do that? You feel in your adolescence that you will probably live forever, and then stuff happens that starts chipping away at that notion. Until the age of twelve, I had never had a cavity. It was a given that when I went to the dentist, there would be no cavities. On the appointment after my twelfth birthday, though, the

X-rays showed that I had nine cavities. Nine. From then on, I assumed that whatever appearance of good luck I had was really like a dam, and that eventually the dam would break and the bad stuff would start happening. Fire would bloom up out of the streets, bodies would fall from the sky.

The fall that my fiancé's mother was diagnosed with stage 4 cancer and terrorists attacked New York and we both lost our jobs, this is exactly what happened. You're not ready for bad things to happen when they do, but they do anyway and then you become ready. Then when more stuff happens, you've got some experience and before you know it, you're a person who can deal. It's sort of like the worst and best thing to be good at.

The longer you live, the more crap is going to happen to you and your friends, and the better you find yourself at handling it, the happier your life will be.

Life always gives us charming juxtapositions. When the sky was falling down around me, I was working hard on an assignment for a fashion magazine about the wonder of fine lingerie. I thought I'd have difficulty wrapping my head around it, but it ended up being a very welcome distraction. I spent hours talking to models on the phone about their particular proclivities in underwear. Unused to being interviewed, they'd take a very long time answering a question, plenty of time for me to doodle a cuckoo clock. One told me how she and her friends went to this superswanky lingerie shop on Melrose Avenue in Los Angeles. They'd go after the store closed, and the manager would blast Duran Duran and provide champagne and . . . I don't remember the food — probably Tic Tacs. And they'd try on different underwear and bra combinations and dance around the store, getting drunk and laughing and spending thousands on stuff that no one would see (or maybe I'm just thinking of my underwear). I was actually very happy to hear about this going on somewhere when I was trying to figure out if I could afford to replace my five-for-five-dollar granny panties. I mean, these models didn't think the world was going to end, and maybe they were right. When I handed in the first draft of the piece, the editor said I needed to go back and get more. There was a gaping, glaring hole in the piece. Where were the *thongs*? I hadn't written about thongs! I was going to have to go back into the field and find a thong wearer. I did my usual mass e-mail to friends asking if anyone wanted to talk to me, and I got an auto-reply from a friend, a beautiful Hollywood producer whom I'd met through my brother. I remember thinking she was the most likely thong wearer, so I was disappointed to read that she was out of the office for an extended period of time. I didn't think much more about it until I got an e-mail from her later in the day from her personal account. She was home on disability leave after being diagnosed with breast cancer, but she was a thong wearer and would be happy to tell me her favorites.

I told her how sorry I was to hear this. I also mentioned that I knew she'd be fine: I had two aunts and a grandmother who'd had breast cancer and went on to live long, healthy lives (it had been thirty-five years for my aunts — and they were still going).

We weren't very close friends, but she wrote me back a long e-mail saying she'd appreciated my supportive words and wanted to hear what was going on with me. I wrote back to her immediately, and — maybe it was my availability or timing — we started to write to each other several times a day. She was beginning chemotherapy and focusing on changing her eating habits. It was huge stuff, but it broke down to being very small. I was not really sure why I was helpful to her, and several years later I asked her. She said it started with the lingerie question. I was asking her something silly and girly and I couldn't see her because it was e-mail so she felt like I imagined her looking as she had before, instead of (her words) "bloated and bald." It meant a great deal to me, helping her at that time, and clearly I was or she wouldn't have been e-mailing me every day. She was hungry to hear about the stupid plans I was making for my wedding — stuff that was far from life-threatening, stuff that really didn't matter. She wanted to hear things that didn't put her in the position of being a sick person.

It's a telling time in one's life, to be called to the plate in that way. The most significant thing I learned in going through it is that every person deals with illness in a different way. People want different things. Some people are pragmatic and unemotional, others may seek spiritual relief or immerse themselves in planning for the future. You know how your friends are, and it's key to be mindful of what they need at those times. It is not necessarily what you would want.

I remember when my mother's good friend Patty was dying of cancer when I was in high school. She had finally stopped chemo and radiation — there was no point anymore. She returned home to her own bed, where she could spend the rest of her time surrounded by family and friends. My mother sat with her in her room, looking at her, filling the silence with talk of the committees they both sat on. Patty interrupted her and asked her to bring over her jewelry box and my mother did. She pulled out a small gold pendant and handed it to my mother.

"Here," she said, "I want you to have this."

My mother brushed it off. "You wear this all the time. I'm not going to take it!"

"I'm not going to be wearing it anymore," Patty replied.

"Oh, sure you will," my mother said in a loud, strong voice. "You're going to get better."

She didn't take it, and Patty died a few days later. It was years after that when my mother told me the story with regret. "She knew she was dying. It probably would've been comforting to her for me to acknowledge that. . . . I was just afraid that she had some small glimmer of hope. I just didn't know."

It's something my friends and I, since we've entered the age where everywhere we look someone has cancer, have discussed at length. How do you act? What do you do?

A couple of years ago I met an old friend, Alice, for dinner. We were friends in college, and she'd since moved to Los Angeles and become a successful television writer. She's a person who can find the funny in everything. When you're around her, your face is in that ready-to-crack-up mode.

We sat down at a booth in a diner in my neighborhood.

"So how is everything?" I asked, ready for some funny celebrity story.

"Oh, very bad," she said, her face serious, no sign that this was a gag. "Jim has cancer."

"Oh, no." Jim was Alice's best friend from childhood. He'd moved to Los Angeles to become a set designer and they ended up living in a house together.

The first thing that runs through my mind when I hear someone has cancer is to ask, "What kind?" It's like when you hear someone's died and ask how old the person was, as if somehow this bit of knowledge will inform your response. "Oh, he has hair cancer? That's not bad." Or "Oh, he was a hundred and twenty? Well, I guess you can't ask for more time than that!"

But this time I didn't ask what kind because the truth is they're all cancer. And I didn't say let me know what I could do. I just said, "I'm sorry," and sat with her and let her talk.

She was considering how hard it was going to be for her. Not in a selfish way — obviously it was worse for Jim. But it's something to think about when you're caring for someone: You need to take care of yourself well enough to be solid for your friend.

Over the next year and a half, I watched Alice handle Jim's illness as only Alice could. I thought and told her many times that if I ever got sick, she'd be the person I would want around. She isn't a person who ever "spins" anything; if you want to know if you look good in a photo or fat or old, Alice will tell it to you straight. When she went with Jim to doctors' appointments, there was frequently dreadful news. It was so terrible that when she heard what they said, she'd realize his condition was worse than she'd imagined. She never said, "Oh, it's going to be okay." She'd say, "Wow, I wasn't expecting to hear that." She told me if you're honest with people, they trust you. She never said, "Wow, this is really bad," to Jim. She told him, and it's the truth, that nobody really knows, and the longer you stay alive the more chance that some new information is coming down the pike.

Even though it seemed impossible, she didn't let the cancer take over their friendship. She made sure to continue doing the things they always did, and talking about the things they talked about. Like joking about other people behind their backs.

Another friend of mine stepped up when she realized that a friend in her office was in the hospital and no one was visiting him. She went to visit every day after work and played cards with him. He was a no-nonsense social worker from the Bronx, and he said, "If you treat me like a sick person, I'm kicking you out." She said at that point it became sort of a joke with them. If she won at cards she'd say, "Pay me now, in case you die before tomorrow." Obviously, you have to know your audience, but he laughed so hard tears came down his face. When he got better he said he believed he might be okay because she was still willing to make fun of him. She didn't get all solemn and morose. She admitted that she didn't know whether it was going to be okay or not, she just knew the way she acted made him feel better. She was relaxed around him. I watched that same friend when her sister got cancer, though, and it was not the same. She was overwrought. When she told the guy she'd been such a comfort to, he said that was why he didn't want his family around when he'd been sick.

Illness is rough and unpredictable. One of my closest friends was pregnant and going through the customary prenatal testing, when it was discovered that her baby was not okay. The prognosis was that it would be born, suffer, and die. It was unspeakably agonizing when she and her husband decided to terminate the pregnancy. Although she knew what was going to happen, she didn't stop taking her prenatal vitamins or abstaining from diet sodas. It was something I knew she'd live through, but the mental anguish was grueling and there was no telling how long it would take her to recover from that.

When she was waiting for the surgery, she didn't want anyone to see her. She didn't want people to see her belly. Even me. So we stayed on the phone together for hours talking and she would cry and then say, "Will anything ever be good again?" In that situation I was relentlessly optimistic. I felt like it was extremely important for her to have her feelings of sadness and grief, but also to know that however consuming they were, she should still have hope.

Toward the end of my pregnancy with Violet, I was diagnosed with preeclampsia.

Preeclampsia is a hypertensive disorder of pregnancy where you get crazy high blood pressure and protein in your urine. Symptoms include swelling, rapid weight gain, headaches, et cetera . . . and it's the leading cause of maternal and infant illness and death. The doctors put me on bed rest and told me to lie on my right side, and every day I was monitored. It was the first time in my life I ever had a serious medical problem. Over the course of my thirty-six years I'd had plenty of medical tests, and I was always fine. And every time I had a test I told myself, "This is it," that some major issue would be revealed, but I kind of did that to trick the gods of deciding who has a disease into thinking that I was prepared so they wouldn't have to give it to me. Because they only like to surprise you. The problem with preeclampsia is I'd never heard of it, so I couldn't prepare for it. My sister-in-law had told me not to read about things that could go wrong in pregnancy because they'd just freak me out, but later I realized if I'd known, the gods couldn't have caught me off guard like that, so I still plan to sue her. There I was with my husband and my mother and aunt all taking care of me, but it was my friends who made me laugh and think of other things.

Jancee said, "What can I do for you?"

I said, "Nothing, I'm fine."

"C'mon! Anything!"

Without thinking I said, "Talk about things that have nothing to do with babies, births, pregnancy."

She read me entire issues of magazines — *Us Weekly* and *InStyle* — over the phone, making appropriate mocking comments when necessary. Anytime she got to a pregnant person (because celebrities do pregnancy differently from us mortals; they wear cute designer clothes and jaunty hats), she'd say, "That jerk Kate Hudson is flaunting her belly all over the place. . . . *Next!*" And we'd move on to a hard-hitting exposé on hobo bags.

It was indeed one of the most important learning experiences in my life, because I found out what it feels like to be seriously ill. Even though it was temporary, it was also potentially fatal, and the stuff I noticed, the stuff that bugged me, were the things I couldn't do. I'd lie on my couch on my right side, because it's better for the heart, and see how messy my apartment was, and look at my undoable to-do list. My mother drove five hours to take care of me and stayed during the week when Paul was at work, and then drove home for the weekends. I was so grateful to her I cried when she left, but on the phone to Jancee, I'd say, "God, it's so messy here!" And Jancee would zip up to my place and clean, and I'd say, "DON'T CLEAN," and she'd say, "I'm not!" as she'd clean. Or she'd say, "I love cleaning, you're doing me a favor." And my friend Lorrie would stop by with a chicken dinner from our favorite takeout place. She told me she didn't cook, because she was worried I'd feel guilty about that, so she just bought dinner.

All of my friends were wonderful. My family was amazing, but I needed my friends, too. I needed people I could be normal with. And maybe people who weren't thinking about me dying.

After I gave birth, the preeclampsia was gone. It took some time to recover, but in a matter of months I was back to full speed, and the really significant lesson for me was a newfound empathy for people who were sick. I had felt the absolute frustration of not being myself. Of going from running six miles a day to not being able to walk across a room without help and tears.

I'm very close to my family, but my friends know a different side of me. In some ways your family always sees you as you were: with the adolescent temper or the bland food palate. You can tell them that you now eat pad thai, but they'll still be shocked when you don't order the cheeseburger and French fries when you meet them for lunch. They're much slower to see you as you are now. Even though you might be paying rent and bills and caring for a family, they still think you sleep with a night-light on. Your friends know you as you are now, and you can complain to them in ways that you wouldn't with your family. (Also, you can complain to your friends *about* your family.)

About three weeks after my preeclampsia had been diagnosed, I got a call from my doctor, who said that day's tests were not good and I should go to the hospital and deliver. It was a few days before my baby shower, which I still consider slightly lucky since the lovely dress I had bought for it wouldn't even marginally zip up the back because of my aforementioned rapid weight gain. The delivery was long and difficult (not one of those champagne-cork births), and a lot of unpleasant things happened. The way the catheter was removed from my hand left it swollen to the size of a football; my feet were so distended I couldn't even fit into my old-man slippers — I had to wear paper hospital shoes; and I had some bizarre allergy to the tape over the stitches on my stomach, so that when it came off I had ribbons of red welts and burns. I was kind of a mess. I couldn't walk upright, and worst of all, I had to go home while my baby stayed in the hospital.

When I came into my apartment, a small one-bedroom, I found that a kind friend had delivered all of my shower presents. They were stacked all around the living room. There was not a pathway of space to walk through. I didn't even look at them and lay on the couch. Jancee came over that night. She had a sweet smile on her face as she came toward me. Through gritted teeth she said, "What the hell is all of this?"

"My shower gifts," I said.

"This is making you crazy, right?" she whispered.

I burst into tears. I was hormonal and tired and I missed my baby, and there was nothing I could do about any of it. But it was my incredibly chaotic, packed apartment that put me over the edge.

"I'm going to go down to the super and get a garbage bin and put in everything here," she said, already gearing up for action, "and we can stick it in storage. You don't need all this stuff, right?"

"I don't even know what it is," I whimpered.

She started hilariously tearing paper off packages — my friend who had no kids and less interest in them than anyone I knew, until a few years later when she had her own most beautiful baby in the world — describing what she thought each item was and why I didn't need it. I laughed so hard I peed on the couch and ripped a stitch. But it didn't matter, because I knew somewhere inside me that things would be okay. I had a friend who could make me laugh and, just for a moment, forget what was happening. God willing, any illness in life passes swiftly, but the friendships that buoy you are blessedly enduring.

CHAPTER 3
MISSED CONNECTIONS

I used to love to watch my daughter making friends when she was a toddler. Wherever we went, she'd find someone around her height and that would be it. The friendship consisted of doing things near each other, not really together, or sometimes grabbing something out of the other one's hand. The point was, she found mates who were at the same place in their life as she was — not great at talking or using the toilet, but very interested in putting things in their mouth. There were no messy breakups; we'd leave the playground or store and she'd have closure.

It does help to be in the same place in life as someone you are friends with; you can be supportive to a pregnant woman when you don't have to look back forty years to your own pregnancy, and maybe the same principle applies if you're both working at the same place or you're both single or both newly married or you both let four dogs sleep in your bed. This system seems to work well, but if you're friends with someone for a long time, there are most likely going to be points where you stray from those parallels. Through elementary school you do have similar lives, but rarely is our existence tidy enough to keep you and your friends in line beyond college.

In the early nineties, I was in my twenties, but being the late bloomer that I am, I like to think of it as my adolescence. I was like a twenty-two-year-old tween. I lived alone and was (sort of) responsible, but I still wasn't convinced that I didn't need a cootie shot before kissing a boy. I wasn't quite "there" yet.

I was visiting my parents in their new house on the border of New York and Vermont in the summer, and a guy from my high school "family" was having a party/ hayride at his grandparents' house not far from my folks. My parents and I decided to go, and of the kids my age, most were boys or girls who played sports really well. I was hanging back, trying to decide if I loved it or hated it, when I was approached by a girl my own age. I admit it, I don't think I started calling girls women until I was well into my . . . okay, never. She was very pretty, and I learned she was the girlfriend of one of my high school friends' college roommates, a guy I quite liked. In a large crowd of people she made a very good joke and I was the only one who laughed. We made our way to each other. Here we were in a big sapphire pool of enormous sailfish, and we were some kind of animal that didn't swim. We later dubbed our meeting "a Jew and a Jersey girl in a WASP's nest." The Jersey girl was Jancee. We had a speed-bonding session and exchanged numbers. She told me she was an editor at *Rolling Stone* and I told her I was a writer for *National Geographic Explorer.* The truth was at the time she was an editorial assistant who put together the Billboard charts in the magazine, and I was a clerk in my dad's insurance company who had done a test script for *National Geographic* that was judged promising.

The following week we made plans to have dinner. She was commuting from New Jersey but looking for an apartment in the city, and I was living on the Upper West Side. Since I was the city girl, I chose the spot for dinner, Kaplan's at the Delmonico — the delicatessen I ate at with my father when I was a kid. It was not the "insiders" spot I would've liked to come up with, unless by insiders you think "old people having dinner at four p.m."

We had a great time, and then we fell in friend-love, talking on the phone several times a day from our respective non-private cubicles, laughing until we wheezed. It was prehistoric times, when people had big Michael Douglas *Wall Street* cell phones, with no texting and no personal computing or e-mail, IM'ing, tweeting, or Facebooking. It was the best of times, it was the worst of times; in order to communicate we actually had to pick up the phone and call each other.

I'd be sitting at my desk in the morning, surrounded by bran muffins and water bottles, and the phone would ring and I'd hear, spoken, "I've been funny, I've been cool with the lines."

Jancee made up a game where she'd speak the lyric of a song and I'd have to guess what it was, which is a lot harder than it sounds. I walked around the office thinking, I know this, dammit! I'd call her back and sing, "Ly-eeeens," but I still didn't know it.

"Give up?" she'd taunt.

"No way!" I'd say, hanging up and working on it longer. I do believe that one of the reasons I had such a hard time getting my life on track in my twenties was that so much of my thinking was devoted to Name That Lyric. Finally, hours later, I'd see Rick Springfield's face in a bathroom mirror and remember it was a phrase from "Jessie's Girl." I would call her triumphantly, and we'd both spend an hour talking about our love of Rick "back in the day." Then we'd update each other on what we'd had for lunch and who in our office was bugging us.

Over time, Jancee became the editor of the "Random Notes" section in *Rolling Stone,* and I was still nothing. She got busier, and we couldn't talk for quite as long as we used to, but I didn't feel left behind because I wasn't. Jancee knew I wrote and assigned me pieces for the section. It was generally about two hundred words, and I'd get maybe a hundred bucks, not credited, but it was still extremely significant to me. I went places and interviewed people as a reporter for *Rolling Stone.* It had cachet up the yin-yang. The very first assignment she gave me was to go to a Rick Springfield comeback concert at Irving Plaza, a small but hip venue downtown. I'd go to the show and interview him after. The place was packed with women from Long Island and New Jersey, somewhere around my age and older. We'd all been in high school in the

1980s when Rick had his hit records as well as his starring role as Dr. Noah Drake on *General Hospital.* I thought Rick must never have imagined he'd be in this place when he was on top; then I realized that nobody there ever pictured this — whatever it was — as our future.

After the show I called Jancee and told her about my profound and unsettled feeling. What if that happened to us? "Get it. Totally," she responded. We had a shorthand — we never said hello, just answered the phone and launched into our observations.

Jancee's next job was at *Us* magazine. She was assigning profiles, and she assigned them to me. I met or spoke to tons of celebrities and wrote little pieces, and my name was under them . . . *by Julie Klam.* Jancee rose up in the editorial ranks like a rainbow kite, and she allowed me to swing from her tail. If not for her, I don't know how I ever would have had a career. Aside from the fact that she had faith in me to complete assignments, she was also there to hold my hand, and I was nothing if not a big fat chicken.

I was never, ever jealous of Jancee. I was proud of her and so grateful that she helped me. Still smarting from my first job at a talent agency where I was yelled at and fired, I didn't really want any more responsibility than the odd piece here and there. Sometimes Jancee would hear of positions at magazines and recommend me for them, and I'd do the interview and not get the job. There was no doubt my ambivalence was evident. But it all worked for Jancee and me until it didn't. I was so in awe of her work ability. She just did what she had to, while I made excuses about why I couldn't. I remember a job came up that she thought I should apply for. It was way out of my comfort zone (long days, late nights, travel . . .). I just didn't want it and she said to me, "Just take it and do it for a couple of years, then you can get something else or quit or whatever."

A couple of years? I thought she was insane, and also wildly ambitious. I explained to her how very long "a couple of years" was and she laughed and didn't press it. I wonder if she was irritated by my stuntedness.

As is often the case, it was a new boyfriend who drove the wedge between us. He was Mr. Snazzy Hipster and Jancee did a little of what I guess is called "partying" with him. No longer interested in meeting me for hot fudge sundaes, she was doing drugs with rock stars. Every so often we'd get together and go shopping, but she was buying pleather pants and I was wearing a dirndl skirt with Reeboks. Oh, how the mighty city girl had fallen. Jancee, who a couple of years before had needed my help to find a dress for an event, was now an über-fashionista club kid, and I was still eating early bird dinners. So we drifted apart for a few years. It made me both angry and sad, but I really didn't have much to offer. Eventually, I left the insurance job to put my energy into freelance writing (and to be a full-time mother to my Boston terrier, Otto). Jancee and I still checked in every so often but it was very uncomfortable.

We were not at the same place at the same time, and it seemed like our friendship was over.

Before I turned fully into Miss Havisham, I got a job on the television show *Pop-Up Video,* thanks to the second person who believed in me, my future husband, Paul. At this time, Jancee was back at *Rolling Stone* and was a veejay on MTV2 as well as a correspondent on *Good Morning America.* Her career had exploded, and mine had stopped being a total embarrassment, so I wondered if we'd be friends again. Her stupid, douchey boyfriend had disappeared, but I didn't really feel like I knew Jancee anymore.

I was sitting in the morning meeting at work when one of the researchers was reading the pertinent music news. It seemed Melissa Etheridge had revealed who the father of her baby was . . . David Crosby. The story was broken on the cover of *Rolling Stone* and written by Jancee. I had no idea about it and was struck by the fact that we were so estranged that something this big could have happened without my knowing. There was a time when Jancee would call me from her gyno's office to ask me the date of her last period. And I knew.

For the years that we had been friends, Jancee had been the successful one and the one with the boyfriend. Now I had a boyfriend and a job so I thought it might bring us together, but then she didn't have the boyfriend (for about ten minutes) so we weren't in the same place again, and we just could not get back on track with our friendship. Over the next few years, Jancee met a guy and got engaged. When she called to tell me, I said, "I am so happy for you." And she cried and said, "I wish this was happening to you and not me." And I cried and said, "I wish it was happening to both of us together, but don't let me ruin this for you. I'll do everything I can to help you."

It turned out that unlike me, Jancee

wanted a destination ceremony with just her immediate family so there was no endless, vomitous wedding planning. That would happen the following year, when I got engaged. After that phone call, we slowly began talking more and discussing what had happened between us, and working very hard to be friends again.

And we were, but it wasn't exactly like before. Jancee was still very career-focused, and although I had a career, I wasn't that sure of it. It always felt temporary to me. Actually, I think by that time I was not working at *Pop-Up Video* anymore: I'd been fired because I was dating a boss — not my fault, but whatever, it's been twelve years and I am so over it, though why did I get fired and he didn't? Anywho, I was working on a game show at VH1 that was not very cool or satisfying and biding my time until I could focus on being a buh-rye-duh. Because that's what I thought would make me happy, and the process, I'm not proud to say, really did make me happy. I loved the flowers and the dresses and the catering and little chocolate favors and really felt like the actual wedding day was almost beside the point. Jancee was a bridesmaid. She couldn't be there for the rehearsal dinner because it was the same night as the MTV Video

Music Awards. At the time I thought she was a little cuckoo. Who would rather be an on-air personality at a huge awards show than be at a buffet dinner at The Country Barn located off Route 9? Seriously, I didn't mind. I loved her, and we were friends again, but I couldn't comprehend her devotion to work. The day of the wedding, she stayed by my side every second, and when I went to the bathroom and wasn't sure how I'd be able to wipe under my full crinoline, she said she'd do it. We laughed so hard no noise came out of our mouths. The blessing was, she didn't have to wipe my butt.

We were great friends and we were both married, but we still were not at the same place. But we realized that we loved each other enough to push through it and stay friends. It was worth it to me to try to see her cockeyed need to work and be successful.

A year after that, Jancee and I had decided to combine our rapier wits and write a screenplay together. We hadn't gotten very far when I found out I was pregnant. I had one friend who'd moved out of the city who had children, but none of my close friends did. And Jancee didn't want kids. She had been the friend over the years who made hysterical commentary about the loud, runny-nosed kids we'd encounter. I was very aware that when my status changed to mother, I did not want to be possessed and lose my friends. But I had so much trouble working with her because I was so unbelievably tired. We wrote together over the phone. I tried to explain to her that I felt like Dorothy in the field of poppies — I just couldn't stay awake — and she'd say, "No problem, let's work for a few hours."

But after, I want to say . . . one page of writing, I'd need to hang up.

"What?" she'd say, laughing, "I lost you already?"

"I'll call you back," I slurred, and passed out. When the first trimester ended, we finished the script and then wrote a joint magazine piece for *O* magazine.

During my third trimester I got very sick with preeclampsia and was put on bed rest; we talked on the phone while I lay on my right side. I was scared and lonely, and my husband was working at a new show that was grueling and demanding with a mean boss. It was not a good time. When I gave birth early I felt like I was on a different planet. Plus, I actually looked like a planet. No one felt comfortable to me, and my cute little baby was like a scrawny martian. I had wondered before if I'd be one of those new mothers who acts like she's in first class and the childless are in coach, but the first year of motherhood was so excruciatingly hard for me, I was jealous of people without children and of their durn freedom and full-night sleep.

Around this point, when the music coming out of my daughter's bouncy seat felt like the sound track of my mental institution, my therapist suggested I join a mother and baby group. The last thing in the world I wanted to do was make new friends at this scary new place in my life, but I went, telling myself that it was *for the baby.* She was five months old and sitting up; clearly she needed some serious stimulation, some baby talk. I went and sat in the circle. The woman running the group told us she had started it because it had been so important for her when she had a new baby to meet people at the same place, and she went on to tell us how those mothers became the best friends of her life. I looked around at this group of strange women with their weird little-old-men babies and I wanted to run, but I stayed . . . because I was too tired to get up. But I was going to try really hard not to make new friends.

There's a whole odd hierarchy of parents and babies having to do with developmental

63

milestones and age. Somehow, if your baby is eight months old and someone else's baby is ten months old, they are better than you. And if you and someone else have babies that are the same age and their baby talks before your baby, they are better than you. My daughter, Violet, was an early walker, so I scored high on that test, but she was a late talker, so one step forward, two steps back. We did make some friends, but the only moms I really clicked with were those whose kids were younger than mine and thus "worse." When the class was done we formed our own group. There was a woman whose son was a month older than Violet and spoke like Dr. Frasier Crane on the radio. A phone would ring and Alan would say, "I hear a phone ringing." And Violet would say, "Bleh ma ma ma ma." I'd pretend she had said something profound and anyone who didn't understand it was a fool. My best friend during that period was a woman whose son was actually a bit older than Violet, and he couldn't do anything. His mother would say, unapologetically, "Listen, he doesn't walk, he doesn't want to, and he may never want to." We decided that when our kids were older we would hide out together, giving them bottles while everyone else's children were getting their driver's licenses.

I found that although there was a certain type of very solid friendship that could be formed by both parties being in the same trench during the shelling, it wasn't the same as the serendipitous bond you form with someone you really like just because you really like them. It hit me hard, when I stopped being obsessed with the number of hours of sleep I got at night, that I really, really missed my old pals.

There were a few other friends, aside from Jancee, with whom I'd lost touch in those first five months of motherhood. None of them had kids, and one of them, Allison, had been trying very hard to get pregnant, without success. I suddenly realized that I hadn't been lobotomized — the person I was before I became a mother was in there. I had interests, or at the very least I was interested in people who had interests, other than children.

I made lunch dates with friends, and of course they asked about Violet and wanted to see pictures and hear about her, but I quickly moved our conversation to the world at large. I didn't need to talk about my baby with my friends. I had other people in my life who wanted to talk *only* about her. What started as me thinking it would

65

make my friends feel more comfortable actually made me feel better. I wanted to hear what was going on away from the changing table, and it turned into a real breakthrough for me. My epiphany was that relating on the ground that had always been common worked. I always felt very good when, years later, after Jancee and Allison had their own children, they said that I was one of the very few friends who didn't "change" when I had my baby or make them feel that they were in some childless ghetto.

In the last two years, I've watched Jancee turn into the most devoted, insane Mom with a capital M. A woman who used to make us move in restaurants to get away from children now says, "I want everyone I know to have babies so I can touch them!" Her work is still very important to her life, but it ain't the moon and the sun anymore. My daughter is now in third grade and I don't obsess about her the way I did when she was a toddler, but I've kind of become possessed by my work. So we changed places (sort of), and though we know at any point it could all change again, we now know better how to maintain our separate "us."

We make sure to ask how everything's going with our work and kids, but we spend equal time on Madonna (God, there is always so much to talk about with Madonna) and clothes and shoes and politics and the people we both know. (We say only very nice things about them, of course.)

There is something to be said for having "breaks" in friendships. Sometimes you find there are things you need to do in your life and a certain friend may not support that change, at that moment anyway. It is very fair to allow people to grow and change, but it's nice to be able to come back home again, too.

CHAPTER 4
THANKS, BUT
I'M FINE . . . REALLY

My father is a big subscriber to health newsletters. If you've never seen one, they are a few pages written by various doctors, offering advice on exercise, eating habits, and vitamin supplements. There is also always a supposedly objective "article" on the discovery of some magic elixir that fixes all that ails you, and the company behind the newsletter just happens to sell it for $39.95. My father collects his newsletters, lovingly labeling them in a three-ring binder. He highlights particularly important passages and rereads them until they're committed to memory. If you're very special to him, you may read them, too. Sometimes he sends them to me with an article, highlighted, on how women can maintain bone health, and a little penciled note on top that says: *Thought you might be interested* and *Pls Ret.* That means read it and mail it back to him or his binder will cry.

He's my dad, so he's allowed to be annoying with his advice-giving — I almost expect it — but what about friends? Is it ever appropriate for a friend to push us toward doing things their way?

Recently I was having lunch with a former coworker, and I asked her what aspects of friendship she finds the most challenging.

"When people don't take my advice," she said, jabbing a corner of quiche with a fork. "That drives me nuts!"

About ten years ago, while she was in college, she found out she had cancer. She battled it and eradicated it. Later, she married an oncologist. Her mother and father both survived cancer and she reasonably feels she's pretty knowledgeable about cancer. When she hears about someone who has it, she very kindly reaches out to them and lets them know she is available to talk. Many times they are grateful for the opportunity to talk with a survivor, though sometimes they don't respond. When they ask, she tells them, in very certain terms, what they must do. Not what they could do. She has a very strong sense — I don't even think she'd call it an opinion — of what must be done. Not everyone agrees, and from knowing several people who've dealt with cancer, the ways they decided to combat it are very personal. Her ideas favor fighting the disease aggressively, medically. On the other hand, another friend of mine survived cancer and fought it in a different way. She used medicine, but she also used a lot of nutrition, Chinese herbs, vitamins, acupuncture, and healing bodywork. She believes this is what worked for her and it's what she recommends. They're both equally convinced of the superiority of their beliefs. They don't understand people not doing as they say — questioning them, in effect. And each one has a convincing argument about why they're right. I have never introduced them to each other. I think of my traditional-medicine-supporter friend as Heat Miser and my Eastern-medicine-advocate friend as Snow Miser, and I don't really want to cause an earthquake, but they are familiar with each other because when one of them starts bitching about people not listening to them, I refer to the other one's beliefs and say, "Well, maybe she prefers more of a Snow Miser approach." Or, "Perhaps she leans toward a Heat Miser ethic." Though this infuriates both of them, they get it. Advice is advice. It's tricky, and in almost every situation I can think of, it's subjective. Particularly medical advice. That's why there is such a thing as a second opinion, and (if you're lucky) insurance companies actually pay for you to get it.

I've talked to these friends about the fact that pushing their "my way or the highway" advice on people isn't really fair. It's fine if you want to offer advice, but you can't be angry at someone for not taking it, unless they come crying to you after learning the hard way that you were right.

Heat Miser's response to this was, "It's a matter of life and death, so that's why I'm pushy." She said if she wasn't sure she was right she wouldn't do it. I have never managed to get through to them, but I've talked to the people who've been angered by their behavior. I know my opinionated friends are coming from a good place, so I have explained that their stringent advice was given with the best intentions.

There is another area of unwanted advice that I've been talking to women about — relationship advice. One friend, Allison, said recently, "If you're going to keep making the same mistake over and over and expecting a different outcome, I'm going to advise you to change your behavior." In other words, if you're going to be stupid, you're going to get yelled at. I think what it comes down to is that we don't want to see our friends get hurt, especially when we can clearly see a world of pain coming down the pike. Allison had a friend, Sherry, who dated one married man after another. Each one said he would leave his wife for her, and each one didn't. Sherry didn't ask Allison her opinion, but Allison gave it, loudly. Allison felt that if she didn't express her misgivings about Sherry's romantic choices, she might have imploded. It wasn't necessary for Sherry to take the advice, but it was important for her to listen.

After college a friend of mine confided in me that she had a crush on my brother and she really wanted to date him. I loved my brother, but more than anyone I knew I could see he was a heartbreaker. He had a way of making a girl feel like she was the only one in the world one minute, and a forgotten candy wrapper the next. "Don't do it," I said. "You'll get hurt." She didn't want to listen to me. She said the heart wants what the heart wants. (So does the stomach, I said, but we don't eat hot fudge sundaes all day long.) She told me it would be fine, and reassured me that if they went out and it didn't work well, she'd be okay. "No, you won't," I said, "and you'll come crying to me, and I don't want to hear it."

I loved my brother, I loved my friend, and I begged each of them separately not to go out with the other. "You know how you are," I said to my brother. "You'll be gone and I'll be left with this mess."

"No," they both said, "this time it's different. We're really in love." Okay, I told them, I can't stop you, but you don't have my blessing. And when it goes wrong, I don't want to hear about it.

They basically both told me to take my advice and shove it up my arse. By the time they began dating, neither of them was even talking to me. And they went on to live out their golden years together and were congratulated by Willard Scott on the *Today* show! Not really. Less than two weeks later they had a predictably stupid breakup.

I waited patiently for my friend to come to me, as I knew she would, and then I screamed, "I TOLD YOU SO! I TOLD YOU SO! AND I DON'T WANT TO HEAR IT!"

She smiled, knowing I was right, and started to complain to me about what my brother had done! "Am I hearing this right?" I said. "I told you that's exactly what would happen and you refused to listen to me. I love my brother, though, and I really can't listen to you talk about him this way." She refused to believe that I was really serious. We didn't talk after that for a long time.

As a person who spent a good nine years struggling with a freelance writing career, I found myself the recipient of a lot of unwanted job advice from a group of people I'll call the Well of Well-Meaning Friends. From the outside, I realize, it looked to these people like I was mostly working at my father's insurance company and leastly doing freelance, but on the inside, I had big plans.

One of my very talented and successful friends (yes, Jancee) could not understand my problem. She was a hardworking journalist who built a career that blossomed into writing books and appearing on TV. When she saw the way I deliberated about a pitch to a magazine, she thought I was crazy.

"Just send it!" she'd bark.

"But what if they assign it to me?" I responded.

"That's what you want!" she said, incredulously.

I was really afraid of work and putting myself out there. I had been fired from my first real job and I was gun-shy. I always sort of felt like Jancee looked at me the way a hedge fund guy looks at a person rummaging through the trash. We were coming from such different places that it just didn't compute. She was never judgmental or harsh with me, but she was constantly recommending me for editorial jobs (the nerve of her!). I'd dutifully go to the job interviews with my paltry writing clips and the people would tell me how great Jancee is and I'd smile and say, I agree. But clearly I wasn't her — or anything like her — because I never got the jobs. It got to the point where I would deliberately wait too long to call about them because I couldn't stand the process. Only I knew that what scared me more than losing the job was getting the job.

"What if I get it and I don't like it?" I'd plead with her.

She said the thing about doing it for a "couple of years."

A couple of years is not a long time if you're trying to build a cathedral, but it's a very long time to be hating a job. Or to have a splinter.

I was reminded of this a number of years ago when my friend Molly got a new job as a literary agent. Her job before that was writing books and magazine pieces and taking care of her three little kids in her very nice apartment. Getting this job was a very big deal! A very swanky party was thrown for her, she got business cards. Two weeks later my friend Deb and I met her for lunch at a fancy Asian fusion restaurant in mid-town.

"I'm expensing this," Molly gestured, "so order well!"

Both Deb and I were at low points financially and it seemed like the most luxurious experience in the world.

"So how is it?" I asked excitedly.

Molly, not one to mince words, said, "I hate it. It's horrible." She looked like she was going to cry.

We ordered and listened to her talk about the horrors of her new job. Insane bosses, ridiculous expectations, long hours. It was so not good.

Deb, who had worked as a photojournalist in war-torn countries, said, "It sounds awful."

"I think I'm going to quit," Molly said.

"Oy," I said, "you should."

"Well, you can't quit now," Deb said, looking at me for backup, as if I was like her. "You've got to give it six months to a year."

"Six months?" Molly wailed. "To a year?"

"Things may improve," Deb explained. "At least you have to attempt to make them better."

"You want to quit now, right?" I said.

Molly put her head on the table and whispered, "I don't want to go back there . . . after lunch."

It was very funny to see Deb and me giving her dueling advice. The woman who jumped on a tank hurtling through Moscow and found her way out of Afghanistan by herself, and the sissy who wouldn't take an apartment because my grocery company didn't deliver there. We were the proverbial angel and devil on her shoulders (the angel wearing camouflage gear and combat boots, the devil in sweatpants and no bra and clutching a takeout menu). Molly knew whom to ask. And to her credit, Deb kept up her argument, thinking she was making complete sense, while for my part I was asking Molly if she wanted me to go up there and quit for her. "I'll do it," I said.

She didn't even make it to the end of the week. And she had my blessing.

While they take a very different form from most advice, setups can feel like the same unwanted hand sticking itself in your business. Around the time I turned thirty, a few of my friends got married, and suddenly it became their life's mission to make sure every other single person joined the coupled fray. I was invited to one of their weddings, a very swanky affair at a Manhattan hotel. I picked up my card for Table 6 and began to

77

look for my seat. When I saw the table, I thought there must be some mistake. There were eight seats, and the seven people already sitting there were all men (or really "guys" — one wore a tie with cartoon characters on it). I wondered if it was clear to all of them that I was the wedding's token Desperate Woman. I sat down and asked who else had their period, and that was pretty much the beginning and ending of me at Table 6.

It wasn't that there was anything wrong with these guys, it was just, Come on! A few days later the bride called me from Antigua to ask if any of them had asked for my number. I said next time she should hide them behind a wall and let me ask them questions about making whoopee in a full-on *Dating Game.* Incidentally, one of them did call me. He was a dermatologist, and after spending the evening gazing at my skin, he thought to ask me if I wanted a discount on Botox. Be still, my heart!

I have never asked anyone to set me up. I had enough trouble figuring out what I wanted for myself, so to think someone else would have a sense of what I wanted was kind of unlikely. Plus, I didn't want to date a stranger. There is something very 1959 about it. It makes me think of my mother and her fabled blind date with Herman Schmegeggy, the undertaker's son. So the blind dates I had (there were three) were forced on me by well-meaning (pushy) friends. Here's the criteria people use when setting up someone. (1) Is he single? (And "single" can also mean unhappily married.) (2) There is no other criterion.

There was one guy friend of mine who was sure I'd love this other friend of his. It was, according to him, a "can't miss." The only reason I considered it was that he said we were the two funniest people he knew, so I was blinded by my gigantic ego. Flatter me and I'll forget my "No blind dates" rule. Also, men rarely act as cupids, so I figured maybe he had some special gift. It certainly seemed worth a shot.

I didn't actually speak to this guy before the date, but he left instructions on my answering machine for where to meet him (a restaurant that serves big game) and described what he looked like (a "Jewish John Travolta"). It's important to note here that many, many Jewish men claim they look like really handsome Italian actors. I've met a self-proclaimed Jewish Al Pacino and a Jewish Bobby Cannavale. And though there may be a fleeting resemblance (dark hair, dark eyes, a wardrobe that dates to the

Saturday Night Fever era), the main thing you notice is that they aren't John Travolta, Al Pacino, or Bobby Cannavale, which I personally find disappointing, and which provides an excellent segue into describing this date. I believe in the right circumstances, this guy could be funny. Like if you've just finished electric shock treatment for depression. No, I'm wrong. My grandfather would've thought he was funny. Because his jokes were peppered with vintage racist terms like "Chinamen" and "Polacks," complete with stereotypes and hideous impressions.

For a short time during the date, he got serious. He wanted me to know about his work. He supplied recycling bins to schools in Lower Westchester. He was the only one who did this. It was his domain. I asked him about it: Were the bins different for schools than for companies? Did Lower Westchester recycle more thoroughly than Upper or Middle Westchester? He told me what he could without breaking his ironclad Hippopotamus Oath. And that was it. He never once asked me about anything I did, even though I had been excited to say I'd just come from interviewing Gordon Gano of the Violent Femmes about his adaptation of *Carmen.* I sort of brought up that I enjoyed my work, too. He absentmindedly said, "Oh yeah, something with Letterman, right?" and then signaled for the check. I just couldn't compete with those damn recycling bins.

At the end of the night, he admitted for us that there was no chemistry, so we should go Dutch. I actually offered to pay for him if he promised not to do a Dutch accent accompanied by a bad joke about wooden clogs.

There's something so deeply insulting about being paired up by a friend who sees you as a match with someone who is so clearly not your match. But mainly, unless you are asked to provide a blind date, setting a friend up is suggesting to a person that there's something wrong with their life the way it is and you have an idea how to fix it. I believe that very few people who really want to be in a relationship can't find one. Just like there are people who are actually happy to not have children . . . or dogs (so I've heard). But I don't think people think that when they set you up. People are indeed trying to help.

Of course if you choose to have a life with friends (or dogs), you are bound to get unwanted advice. I get it all the time. In my old neighborhood, no matter what the weather, a casual friend who lived in my building would consider it her duty to stop me every day to tell me my baby was underdressed, or getting too much sun — the basic message was that my daughter was in some way not cared for properly. Now I live in a different neighborhood, and Violet is older, but there's a new woman I'm friendly with who regularly tells me my dog Bea is shivering . . . or she's so hot that she needs water immediately. I'm sure all of this attention is very well meant. Right?

I do believe giving advice is a — maybe at times misguided — form of showing care, as much as we might chafe at it. If you look at where it's coming from, a loving place, and take it with a modicum of grace, you can allow your friends to care for you. And as my mother says, God willing, you'll live long enough to give them unwanted advice right back.

CHAPTER 5
MY FRIEND HAS GONE NUTS

I'm crazy. No two ways about it. I mean, I'm a high-functioning nut. A tax-paying, pants-wearing, law-abiding (except for the stupid ones) citizen. I shower and brush my teeth and present normally, but inside I'm a few clam strips short of a combo platter.

Because of that, I think I'm fairly tolerant of people's quirks. If my friend Patty, for example, could avoid ever eating in public, she would. Really. She has zany restaurant habits. She drinks iced tea with about ninety-three packets of artificial sweetener and thirty-two lemon wedges. Despite this, she also happens to be extremely popular and successful. I've had dinner with her a million times (broiled fish, no oil, no sides, or an egg-white omelet with no oil and "herbs if the chef wants to put them in, but it doesn't matter to me"). It's an ongoing quirk and one that I accept lovingly and without criticism, even though I feel like a pig in a trough when I eat with her, because it's part of being a friend. I think if I went through all of my friends, I could come up with at least one trait for each that would make you say, "Jeez, that's kinda out there." And probably at least ten for myself.

I was on a plane, seated next to a woman whom I instantly fell in friend-love with because she was wearing a Halloween sweatshirt and Halloween is my favorite holiday. And it turned out she had handcrafted it herself! It had appliquéd little pumpkins and ghosts and witches on it and a big yellow moon. There were sparkles! There were studs! The black kitty's tail was fuzzy! After my effusive complimenting, we settled down into normal non-talking-on-an-airplane mode. She kept glancing over at a magazine article I was reading, with pictures of bottles of colored water. Finally she couldn't stand it anymore.

"I beg your pardon," she interrupted, "whh-at is that about?"

"Oh," I said, "they're talking about different cleanses."

"Oh!" she said, getting it. "Those are cleansers!"

"Actually, *cleanses,*" I corrected. "For the body."

"Oh, cleanses, like for your face and stuff?"

"No."

"Oh, like the skin on your body?" She so badly wanted to understand this very troubling concept.

"It's, uh, inside-the-body cleanse."

She looked at me so desperately wanting to say, "Ohhh." But she couldn't.

"It's this thing," I continued, "people, mostly women, do. . . . It's sort of like a detox of your organs, I guess. You lose weight, and like, your skin is really clear, I think. I haven't actually done one."

"Does the inside of these people's bodies get very dirty?" she asked, trying so hard.

"Apparently," I said, and smiled.

She went back to eating her human-head-sized braided, glazed, chocolated, cheesed, powdered-sugared Danish and drinking her coffee with cream and sugars. In her world, the cleanse was crazy, but in cleanseland that pastry would be certifiable.

And you know what? That's what makes this country great; we have cleanse people, pastry people, and a hand-detailed Halloween sweatshirt. Though I live in Manhattan, where people go to extremes in the name of beauty, I still get alarmed when anyone seems to be taking it too far.

I met my friend Leesa several years ago at the gym. Just talking while waiting for the StairMaster one day, we realized we had lived somewhat parallel lives, though ten years apart. She was actually born ten years and two days before me. I have one child, a daughter who is eight; she has one child, a daughter who is eighteen. We both went to New York universities and have lived on the Upper West Side ever since. We've gone for coffee a few times, but we mostly talk at the gym. I really enjoy her company. Our parallels end, though, in that she is a former model and looks like Venus incarnate.

She's a soothing type, and when I met her I was in complete New York City parent angst about my daughter's school prospects, which were unspeakably grim. At four it appeared she was doomed for a lifetime of failure because she hadn't made it into one of the highly sought-after lottery schools.

I spilled my guts to Leesa, tears pouring down my face, and she comfortingly explained that while it always seems this way, it does work out. She made some really good suggestions, mainly that I should do what I could and then keep following up, be an advocate, and if I was tenacious, I'd find myself in the right place at the right time and Violet would get a break. It almost seemed like she was psychic, because a week later I was doing my follow-up calls and one spot opened up in a perfect school and I swear I saw rainbows stretching across the sky and fairies popping out of little hearts.

I was indebted to her for her kindness at that moment, and somehow in my head I linked her with Violet's getting into the good school.

We always had nice chats after that, and one day I saw her at the gym looking very distracted. She asked me if I wanted to meet her for coffee after the workout; she just wanted to talk. I agreed. Before even sitting down she started talking about this new injectable. (Boy, I miss the times before that was a word.) She wondered if I'd noticed her looking different. I scrutinized her face for something. Other than her worried expression, she looked as gorgeous as ever to me.

She whispered, "I'm going to be fifty-four this year."

I know, I said, because I was going to be forty-four.

"I have been *thickening.*"

"What do you mean?"

She whispered again, "None of my clothes fit."

Before this, I had never heard her talk

about her looks at all. She wasn't vain, and she certainly wasn't one of those women who walk around the locker room naked for way longer than necessary. She hardly wore makeup, and I'd never heard her mention Botox or Restylane, and having seen her week after week, I'd never witnessed any telltale black eyes or bruises that are signs of plastic surgery. She wasn't just gorgeous, she seemed to have amazing genes as well. We had both laughed at the absurdity of Jancee's *Vogue* story about women who had pinkie toes removed so their feet could fit better into Manolo Blahnik and Christian Louboutin shoes.

I told her that everyone has those feelings, but that she was beautiful and thin and if she had put on a pound or two, only she would notice it.

She nodded, unconvinced, and I told her the Catherine Deneuve quote about how as women age they have to choose between the face and the ass — only one of them can look good. It made her laugh and she started asking about Violet.

After that, I noticed that she was at the gym every time I was there, arriving before I got there and remaining after I left (and I stay for an hour and forty-five minutes). When we talked, all she would do was tell

me about some new bizarre hormone re-
placement therapy or this thing they have
only in Sweden, or show me pamphlets
about experimental drugs — one was called
the Fountain of Youth, only "fountain" was
misspelled, and another was called Magical
Youth Elixir. ("Elixir" is a big word in the
youth industry; it's like the stuff they drink
in *The Hobbit,* I think.) She got crazier and
crazier and then finally did start looking different. Her face was puffy one day, like
she'd had some allergic reaction to one of
these things. She started railing about the
FDA's not approving her preferred treatments because they wanted to keep women
down (?), and when I suggested there was
something slightly alarming about how
much of these things she was "doing," she
got very mad at me. She said she thought I
would understand and that I was going to
get old, too, and then I would be wishing
I'd paid attention to her. She didn't speak
to me again after that, and very ceremoni-
ously avoided me, until I started to feel like
I had done something wrong. A few months
later she disappeared from the gym al-
together, and I was sorry. I totally related to
her fear of aging and her wishes that things
could be different, and though I have yet to
do anything, I confess I haven't ruled it out

89

(though the cautionary tale of the woman writer who died getting a face-lift has kept me pretty far from the hospital). In fact, I think I reacted to her behavior because I have the same fears. I had looked to her as someone who was aging gracefully and caring more about the inside than the outside. She did what was reasonable, and then suddenly it was all too much and she went off the deep end. Would that happen to me? I probably could have engaged her more on that level instead of jumping to the "You're acting crazy" gambit. I might have actually reached her, and maybe we both could have gained something from the experience.

When we see that a friend seems to have gone round the bend, it's important to ask: Are we talking temporary insanity or the long-term kind? Is it something we can help with, or are we better off giving our friend space to figure things out?

I personally like to pepper my life with eccentric types. It really makes my world a much more interesting place. I know when I see Bernard, an artist, in the park, I'm going to have a story to tell. Bernard wears spats, a bow tie, and a straw boater — your typical "dandy." He was telling me stories about the people he used to run around with, and in one of the stories he mentioned

J. P. Morgan. I went home and looked through a biography of the famous banker, and I realized that for Bernard to have known him he'd have to be at least 115 years old. So he embellishes the truth a bit. But he's harmless. I'm not making him the executor of my estate or anything. Though I definitely would invite him to a party.

When I was in college one of the friends in my little pack of misfits started acting weird. His roommate told me he was doing some very odd things, like obsessively emptying the pencil sharpener, and getting really mad at the friend for throwing away an old moldy orange in their fridge. I noticed things, too. He was distracted and agitated. When we all went to a movie on campus one night, he had a fit because one of the guys forgot his glasses and we were all forced to sit closer to the screen. In short, he was not fun to be around anymore. Everyone was annoyed afterward, and the consensus was we needed to lose him. "Just don't anyone tell him what we're doing anymore," one guy announced.

That didn't sit well with me, and I went to his room the next morning and talked to him. He very quickly told me his parents had just announced they were divorcing, and he was miserable. Over the next few weeks I succeeded in persuading him to talk to a counselor at school. Sometimes people in pain don't know what they need or how to get help, and they act out. As a friend, you can direct them. It's important to know that you can support a friend and also to know when it's more than you can or should handle.

Sometimes, though, a friend gets obsessed with something and you think the friend might just drive you crazy. Like, have you ever had a friend who started doing yoga and really loved it? I mean really loved it, like life-changing, mind-altering, you must try this? Has that friend done headstands in your living room when your parents were over? And no matter how many times you tell the friend you aren't flexible, she tries to force you to join her cult of yoga-doers, possibly on a retreat to Central America? What is it about yoga? I hate to sound like the dear departed Andy Rooney, but that is how I feel when I hear about how much I need yoga. Even as I write this I feel my defensive hackles rising. I have only so much time for myself, and I choose to work out at a gym. Also, I once did yoga and the room was so hot I couldn't breathe. And I am not good at it! I can't do any of the poses except the corpse! I'm not naming names, but this friend of mine I'll call Mahatma discovered yoga less than a year ago, and I think if she says the word "ash-tanga" one more time I'm going to leap out the window. She quotes her favorite yoga teacher as though she is one of the great philosophers of our time. Suddenly she drinks out of water bottles with the om sign on them and sits on the floor in a piranha pose (I just made that one up). I know, it's harmless, it's not hurting anyone . . . except me. I am convinced, though, that she will eventually calm down. In the mean-time, AAACCCKKK! SHUUUUUUUT UUUUUUUUPPPP!

Yoga practitioners may not be my cup of chai tea, but animal rescuers are. Many animal rescue people have a little crazy run-ning through them, but not my friend Anna-belle, a greyhound rescuer. She's as normal as a one-dollar bill. When I met her over coffee last fall, she was trying to figure out what to do about her close friend who seemed to be losing it to rescue.

The woman, Charlie, had gone through a very painful divorce. She was in bad shape when Annabelle suggested she join her rescue group as a way to do something that would make her feel better. Charlie had a small house in New Jersey with a fenced-in yard, two greyhound rescues of her own, and somewhere between five and a million cats. She was always willing to take in a foster and sneak out under cover of night to rescue some racing dog who'd run out of time. Annabelle had said she wasn't a big computer user; she had one only at work, and that was where she posted to their Yahoo! group list. Her postings were always in the form of a long diatribe about evil people (mostly men). I'd read some, and in true psycho fashion, her spelling was very poor! To me that's a signal to send for the white coats above all else.

But the problem wasn't her spelling; the problem was that she'd stopped taking the rescues that came in through her group and started "rogue rescuing" and keeping all of the dogs. The term "animal hoarder" was bandied about. No one was sure how many animals she had.

Charlie had found volunteering with greyhound rescue to be the first gratifying experience she'd had since her divorce. It became somewhat consuming for her, but to people in a rescue group, who are frequently exhausted, new enthusiasm is very welcome, so her obsession initially went unnoticed. She worked a nine-to-five job in a big insurance company and was able to come home at lunchtime to let out the dogs and care for them. At some point she got into a fight with one of the people in the group about a rule she broke — she had a non-approved friend of hers holding a dog for her — and from then on she was less involved — *with them.* She still went to shelters and pulled animals, something she was doing under the guise of being in that particular greyhound rescue group, but what she was doing was not actually sanctioned by the group. Annabelle knew it was happening, but she was reluctant to do anything about it because Charlie was her friend, and in her mind the dogs were only being helped. Whatever her personal issues, Charlie was a huge animal lover.

And then things began to slip. Charlie called Annabelle about a German shepherd who was supposed to be put down. He was quite old, his owner had passed away, and he was totally freaked out. He had bitten someone in the shelter and was clearly despondent. The shelter staff had decided that given how miserable he was (and the biting), re-homing him would just prolong his agony. These are very tough calls to make. Charlie wanted Annabelle to help get the dog, and to her credit, Annabelle went to the shelter to see him. She said she'd never seen a dog so crazed. She couldn't get anywhere near him. As difficult as it was to say, she didn't really disagree with the shelter's call. These were kind people, and it wasn't a cramped, city-run shelter that just badly needed the extra space. When Annabelle tried to explain it to Charlie, Charlie got belligerent and hung up. The next thing Annabelle knew, Charlie had talked the shelter into letting her adopt the dog. That was when Annabelle called me.

"I'd go over there and see what's going on," I suggested. "If you're worried, I'll go, too."

She said she'd go herself. She called me that night and told me what she'd seen.

"I could hear dogs barking from a block away." She was anxious and out of breath. "I lost count at fifteen dogs, and the dog she just pulled, the shepherd, was just running around in circles. There was crap everywhere. It really frightened me."

Apparently, Charlie's neighbors had already contacted authorities and Charlie had to get rid of all but her own dog by the end of the week or they'd be removed. She was pleading with Annabelle to help her avoid getting all the dogs put back in the shelter, so now Annabelle was scrambling to get as many people as she could to take the dogs into foster care.

When it was all settled, Annabelle met Charlie for coffee. She thought the friendship was pretty much over, but to Annabelle's surprise, Charlie was contrite and grateful to her friend for her help. She apologized for the mess and confessed that the county had said she was no longer allowed to have any dogs except her own; the county would be monitoring her. When I spoke to Annabelle, she was feeling very bad for Charlie. We both said that it was something we could see happening to us if we found ourselves in the kind of rough emotional state Charlie had been in. I suggested she offer to take Charlie's dogs for a weekend so Charlie could get away for a break. She did and it worked out very well. (Believe it or not, Charlie went on a yoga retreat . . . *twitch.*) It's important to remember that people can go off the deep end; it doesn't mean they have to stay there. And when they come back, it's nice to have a friend waiting with a warm towel.

CHAPTER 6
THREE'S COMPANY

No adult can keep up with the ins and outs
and intricate rules of kids' relationships. I
remember telling my mother when I was in
junior high that you could no longer simply
"date" people like she did in her day. The
way things worked now, I informed her, was
that upon your first meeting with a guy you
were "going out" exclusively — what she
still anachronistically referred to as "going
steady." Or you weren't with this person at
all. There was nowhere in between.

There is no point in trying to prove the
stupidity of these rules to the kids who
know and follow them, because it's like *Lord
of the Flies* and you just don't have the
conch. So when Violet explained to me that
it was out of the question in second grade
for her to be friends with two girls at the
same time, I took it seriously and didn't
argue. Apparently, if Susie and Mary are
friends and Betty tries to play with them, it

will be assumed that Betty, the interloper, is trying to "friend-steal" Susie or Mary, or spy on them for the evil Dotty. It was all okay because Violet was best friends with Maya, a hilarious, very strong-willed little girl who liked to take care of Violet. She promised Violet that if anyone was mean to her, she would punch them in the nose, even if it meant going to juvie. All was right in the land until a couple of weeks before Christmas, when Violet found out that Maya was leaving to go to another school after the holiday break.

Without Maya, Violet was lost. She couldn't make a new friend because everyone already had a friend, and she ended up playing alone for about a month. I was heartsick about it, but I couldn't really do anything except talk to her about how she felt. Then one day, a little boy in her class named Jacob came up to her (breaking the rule against boys talking to girls) and said, "Violet, you look sad."

"I *am* sad," she told him.

"Is it because Maya moved away?"

"Yes," she answered. "And now I have no friend."

He took her hand and said, "I'll be your friend."

So her year was saved by the kindness of Jacob.

But what was this about a one-friend-at-a-time rule? It's one thing when you're on a date and you want to make out — a third person is, in fact, "crowding." But what's wrong with the dynamic when you're platonic friends?

I think in Violet's class it was just hard for them to figure out how to share three ways. Two was much easier to negotiate. This all disappeared in third grade, when suddenly groups of three were in vogue. It even became the style to share a Best Friends heart necklace that had three parts. It read "Best Friends Forever," so each kid would have more than one letter.

It is unquestionably harder to attain intimacy with more than one friend at a time. It's much easier to confide in one person at a time (unless you like to air your grungies on national TV, in which case intimacy is not your goal). Holding a conversation with more than one friend at once at a gathering sometimes reminds me of group therapy, where people would be concerned if they hadn't had a turn talking. It can be harder to navigate.

My good friend Molly must have been a shtetl yenta in a past life. She loves putting friends together who she feels will hit it off. When you talk to her she'll stop listening at some point and start staring through you and suddenly say, "You know who you'd love?" She has a good sense about it because often I already do love the people she means to introduce me to. She throws little parties at her apartment inviting Manhattan women writers, very few of whom know one another beforehand. She serves cupcakes, the international baked good of friendship, and will walk around and say, "Julie, did you talk to Cindy? She likes dogs, too." Or "Cara, you and Debbie are both from the Midwest. You should talk about mushroom soup casserole." People enjoy it; it's like speed dating without having to imagine what your children will look like.

As adults, it's much more manageable for us to mix friends. For one thing, our lives are so busy that a lunch with one person can seem like an unaffordable luxury time-wise, especially when people are traveling to visit. A group get-together is a very different dynamic, but it can be useful, especially if you all know one another. It also depends on whether or not your gathering has an agenda. If you are meeting a friend who needs to talk about her failing marriage or problems with her kid's school, that's a duo only.

I was never a fan of introducing friends to each other, for many reasons. The most obvious being, what if they like each other better than they like me? Then I'd have to go out and get drunk and call them at all hours, slurrily sobbing, "How could you do this to me after all I've done for you?" So yeah, that's the obvious reason.

The not-so-obvious reason is that when you have two friends you really like and they do not like each other, it gets awkward. Maybe they don't like each other because they are wondering which one of them you like better. Or whether you've ever told this close friend something they've told you. I always assume there is lots of intrigue going on, even if mostly no one is thinking anything except if there is blue cheese in the Cobb salad.

Maybe it's me, but I've had many post–Meet-my-other-great-friend phone calls that went like this:

ME: Isn't Lulu great?
FRIEND: Really?
ME: Oh, you didn't like her?
FRIEND: Oh, no, I liked her, I was just surprised by her, that's all.

ME: Surprised? By what?

FRIEND: I don't know, she was just not what I was expecting.

ME: You didn't like her.

FRIEND: No, I liked her. I just thought you said she was hilarious.

ME: You didn't think she was funny?

FRIEND: Not really. I mean, the salad thing was kind of funny, but you know, I think it was from *Seinfeld.*

ME: Oh, really?

FRIEND: Also, you didn't tell me she had two-toned hair. Kind of a little . . . I don't know . . .

ME: What?

FRIEND: You know, just trying a little . . . I don't know . . . too hard. (*Under her breath, in a funny voice,* "Rocker chick.")

ME: Oh, I don't know. I like her, but you know, whatever, not everyone likes everyone else.

FRIEND: I mean she was fine.

ME: (*defensive*) Well, you know, I wasn't introducing you so you'd know someone else who is "fine," but it's fine. There's no law that says if I like someone you have to like them, too.

(*Awkward pause, subject switched to Nicole Kidman's unmovable face.*)

OR

ME: So, what did you think of Lulu?

FRIEND: OMG. She was *great!*

ME: Right?

FRIEND: Okay, first of all she is so f'ing funny. I mean that bit with the salad — I was like almost peeing my pants!

ME: I know, she's very funny . . . with vegetables.

FRIEND: Also, I like loved everything she wore. I totally want to go shopping with her. I want that shirt, those brown jeggings — what material was that? Oh, and her boots. Do you know where she got those boots?

ME: She mostly shops online.

FRIEND: (*pause*) Do you think I'd look good with two-toned hair?

ME: (*pause*) Maybe . . . you know, but it might look like you're trying too hard.

FRIEND: Yeah. I'll ask her. We're meeting for drinks tonight.

ME: Oh, that's great. (*Hangs up phone, screams at heavens, "*AAAUUUU-UUUUUUGGGGGGGGGHHHHHHHH-HH!!!!!!!!!!!!!!!!!!!!!!!!!*"*)

I've always felt there was something mystical about three friends — like the Weird Sisters in *Macbeth*, *The Witches of Eastwick*, or *Charlie's Angels* — but when I tried it out as a kid, it turned out not to be the case. One summer I decided to skip camp and just have friend dates. I ended up spending most of my time with two girls I will call Snotty and Bitchy. I would like to say that we all switched off ganging up on one of the three of us, but I think you can probably imagine from the setup that I was the only one who got ganged up on. Snotty and Bitchy did take turns setting me up, playing Snotty cop, Bitchy cop. Snotty would call me on the phone and try to get me to say mean things about Bitchy, whom I could hear breathing on the other extension. The only positive thing to come out of it is that I recently found their pictures on Facebook, and let's just say, they had no portraits in the attic.

A couple of years ago I wrote an essay for an anthology that was edited by the writer/icon Erica Jong, who is known for having written *Fear of Flying*. I did some touring with her, and inevitably during every question-and-answer period someone (always a man, always with a wiry comb-over) would ask Erica, "How do you feel about open marriages?"

An open marriage, I've learned, is where the husband and wife are allowed to date. Sometimes there is another person regularly in their relationship.

"Oh" — she waved it away — "it doesn't work. Someone feels left out and gets jealous." She added, "Feelings get hurt. It's human nature."

With best friends it's kind of the same way; you just can't introduce a new person without one person (me) saying, *"What was wrong with just me? Was I inadequate? Do I need an understudy? Are you planning on having me killed off?"*

If you meet two people around the same time, the platonic threesome dynamic works. And you can go from the three of you to two and back and it's all fairly cool. You are each at the same level to begin with so it isn't a big leap.

Laura, Ann, and I all met online around the same time. Ann and I met for lunch, and Ann and Laura met for lunch. Laura lives in Boston, Ann lives in Connecticut and has a place in Manhattan, where of course I live, but Ann's kids go to college in Boston so she goes there on occasion. So even though Laura and I had yet to meet in person, we somehow thought of each other as three friends together. We also all knew a bunch of the same people, which gave us an instant shared frame of reference.

Laura and I finally met at a party at Ann's

Connecticut house, and we experienced that magical connection in real life, too. About a month or two later, Laura was coming to New York for work, and Ann came into town and we all met up at Ann's for the evening. I felt like there had to be some unique astrological planetary alignment going on because the dynamic worked so well. We each told stories and the others laughed. There wasn't any interrupting, and the proper support was evenly given. We all felt it. If I had brought one of those three-way Best Friends necklaces that Violet and her friends had, I would have gotten it out right then and there. During the evening Ann brought up that she had this radio show she wanted to quit but if the three of us did it together, she'd stay with it. And we did, and it has worked because we have a good three-way chemistry. We also are uncannily always bothered by the same things.

My own wariness at being the third wheel certainly stems from being one of three children — the one whom the other two hated. And then I had two best friends who were sisters and ended up dumping me. Three hasn't always been a magic number for me.

And that's particularly true for the third-wheel scenario. When I was single, I spent a good many years having friends with boy-friends. There was always the point where we would all meet and I'd do my best to be charming and laid-back. I don't think I always succeeded. It feels like it brings out all of the above issues in relief. The worries of the boyfriend and the friend liking each other are multiplied because most likely they're not going to be able to avoid seeing each other.

When I dated the mobster, I wanted my best friends to meet him so they, too, could bathe in the magic of his psychopathology. My friend Barbara came to my apartment and he was there. She has never been one to suffer fools gladly, and her distaste for him was palpable, at least to me. (He was a meathead, so he didn't notice.) He asked her if she was single. She reluctantly said yes, and he said, "I'll find you someone."

Barbara grimaced and said, "No thank you."

"C'mon," he said, "what's your type? You like a guy from a good family?"

She looked at me warily. "I guess so."

Except he wasn't talking about a loving mom and dad and their 2.3 kids; he meant the Gambinos . . . or the Luccheses . . . those kinds of families.

She turned around and climbed up into

my loft bed to read. Every so often he would shout a question up to her and she'd snort a response.

When Jancee met him, she was very polite and acted like all the nutty stuff he said was normal. At the time she was also seeing a questionable guy, though compared with my boyfriend, he was Prince William. Still, that's how she is — she can adjust to being around anyone. I didn't care if Barbara or Jancee passed judgment on him, though, which is a good indicator of how I felt about him and how long I expected him to be around.

When I introduced Paul to my friends, however, and Barbara was sort of coolish to him at first, it upset me and caused a rift between us for a time. But ultimately we worked it out. I think it's sometimes just a matter of getting used to a change. No one likes it at first, especially if it isn't of their own orchestration.

It's very hard to come out and say, "I'm jealous and I feel like I'm about to be replaced." Instead, it's easier to act mad or hurt or busy, and if you observe this in a friend, it's important to go in there and say something reassuring, because we all get insecure, and while you might not want to come right out and say, "I like you better and you'll never be replaced," you can respect and address your friend's feelings, and sometimes that's all it takes.

Success in a "three-way" friendship hinges on realizing the issues that come up among three friends are different from the issues that come up with two friends. Someone can feel left out, or someone else can be jealous, but all of it is fine and totally workable as long as you all have awareness and willingness to see it through. As Violet and her friends know, being close with more than one friend at a time can have its challenges, but you might earn a third of a heart necklace in the process.

CHAPTER 7
FROM @FRIENDS TO IRL

At various times in my twenties I liked to look through the back of *New York* magazine and scour the personal ads. *New York* magazine was for New Yorkers who were literate, busy — all the qualities I'd use to describe myself . . . except the busy part. As cynical as I was about dating, I did secretly hope to find one of the ads winking at me like That Girl in the window. I looked for one — just one — personal ad that didn't use the same clichés as all the others. Some oft-repeated ones included "Can go from jeans to black tie," "On Sunday you'll find me reading *The New York Times* in bed with bagels from Zabar's," and my favorite, "Lover of life!" The people ranged physically from your average "head-turners" to former models, and every fourth ad-placer was "private-jet rich." The men in their thirties and forties were looking for women in their twenties; the men in their fifties and sixties wanted women in their thirties, and everyone insisted on slimness. I figured these people weren't meeting anyone because they were floating around in a fabulous orbit and speaking a language only goddesses and dogs could hear.

It was a huge advancement when the ads started to include a photo, though hardly anyone chose to use one, and even more of a technological marvel when the personal ads launched a voice-mail service. You could call to hear someone's actual voice!

Once or twice I circled an ad, but I always stopped short of answering them, partly because of my own insecurity. I was definitely the right age — that is, much younger than any of the older men trying to secure dates through this service — but I worried I was merely "trim" and not "slim." Would my dates bring a tape measure? Maybe if I skipped dessert a few more times I'd whittle my waist down to less than twenty-five inches.

Insecurity about my looks, however, was not the only roadblock to my love connection. I also had the nagging fear of being bludgeoned to death à la *Sea of Love,* but the number-one reason for my not answering an ad was that if I met someone, I'd have to tell my grandchildren that Grandpa and I met through a personal ad. How mortifying! It was so much better to live life alone in my studio apartment with my Lean Cuisines and five-pound arm weights.

A few years later, Al Gore invented the Internet and there was a new way to meet not only potential mates but friends: "chat rooms." You could chat with virtual strangers online. I did not do this because the person I learned about chat rooms from was a guy in my office who was in his late forties who lived in his mother's attic, wrote werewolf poetry, and howled in the men's room. What can I say? I didn't think I could possibly meet anyone I had anything in common with anywhere he might be hanging out.

Sometime after that, when social networking sites became popular, I scoffed at them, too. "What kind of a loser does one have to be to get a social life online?" (Turns out I was the exact kind of loser!) My neighbor Margaret, an intelligent, funny artist, somehow persuaded me to join Facebook, which I did with a good deal of eye-rolling.

For a very long time I had three friends: Margaret, my brother Matt, and my cousin Sherrie. Sherrie, who had something like forty friends, told me I was an embarrassment to the family and to start friending others or she'd unfriend me. I laughed at this friend-as-a-verb world. Then suddenly I had only two friends. Matt unfriended me.

Dismayed, I ignored Facebook and joined Goodreads, a book networking site where you compare your reviews of books with other people's. This was much less unseemly, more like reading personal ads in *The New York Review of Books* as opposed to the *New York Post*. As an author, I had a professional rationale for participating, and it was also handy to keep track of all the books I'd (claimed to have) read. I got my first Goodread friend request from a guy named Patrick, who worked at a bookstore in Los Angeles and had written something nice about me on the store's blog. Lovely. I would want to be friends with him if he didn't live three thousand miles away. Then he requested me as a friend on Facebook. Aha. Something clicked. The point of Facebook was to be virtual friends not with my next-door neighbor and brother whom I talk to on the phone, but with people I knew in some way but did not often have an opportunity to connect with in person.

In the next year, the media started taking notice, and every professional suddenly needed a "Web presence." You wondered about people you couldn't find on Google — did they exist? For authors who work all day in their bunkers, unshowered and sweating and stinking of self-doubt, Facebook and then Twitter became a way to interact with the world at large — readers who might like your work, and friends who might just keep you from writing that paranoid manifesto. On social media, you could remain in your airstream, but the Internet would present you as that gleaming author photo spouting bon mots. After all that hesitation, I liked it almost immediately. I was happy to be able to take a break and join the virtual water cooler and chat with some of the smartest and funniest people out there. The part of me that grew up in a world where you dialed four digits on a phone to reach a neighbor couldn't believe — and still can't — what's at my fingertips.

I found that as I Facebooked and tweeted more, some of my virtual friendships would get closer, like a friendship does in real life. Still, there was a comfort and safety in the space between us. I wondered about meeting people in real life. A part of me thought the whole point was not having to leave my apartment, but I also wanted more. I did worry that the in-the-flesh versions wouldn't measure up — other people's, but especially mine. I mean, in real life, I don't rewrite what I'm about to say until it reaches maximum wittiness level. It just comes out. Also, my human face has a lot of expressions and many of them are distasteful.

I wasn't looking for romance, so the physical differences didn't matter to me in the least. I assumed that everyone, like me, chose to show the most flattering version of themselves from their best days. I wasn't worried about the other people, I worried about myself being a huge disappointment. While I don't judge people's appearances, I do assume everyone's judging mine (see under: Nuts).

I first "crossed over" into real life when I had a very funny back-and-forth with a writer and book critic on Facebook. Her name was Lizzie and we had many friends in common, so I felt secure that she wasn't going to drug me and Sharpie a mustache on me and post the pictures on our pages. It was very exciting and we announced on Facebook that we were meeting IRL (In Real Life).

If you're not a big Internet user, the one thing you need to know is that people lo-o-o-o-ve acronyms/abbreviations. I hate them and pretty much refuse to use them, mainly because the most common ones are not things I would ever actually say. I don't say Laugh Out Loud (LOL) or call my child

Dear Daughter (DD), plus I think these abbreviations very quickly lead to people attempting to communicate with a big string of undifferentiable clichés. I will shorten words or type "2" for "to" or "4" instead of "for," but that's really more of a lingering Prince influence than Internet parlance.

So Lizzie and I met, and we ended up becoming good friends. The first time we had lunch together we spoke mostly about the weirdness of the meeting and that our voices were not what we imagined. She's about ten years younger than I am so there was no airbrushing that was missing from her live presence. She looked just as pretty as she did online.

Little by little I met more people, but only people I had some kind of real-life connection to. Someone I knew had to have met them face-to-face. Most of them were book industry people, and we reasoned that if there was more socializing in our world, we'd have met in a "regular way."

Patrick, the bookseller from Goodreads and Facebook, introduced me to the joys of Twitter. He did a little interview with me on Twitter about my book so I could get a few followers, showing me that it could be professionally helpful. But the friendship aspect of Twitter ended up being so much more powerful than its professional impact, and it wasn't at all what I expected.

In essence, my reaction to meeting any new people for a very long time was like cavemen throwing rocks at the moon. If you were okay, I'd already know you. And if you want to make friends with me, what the hell is wrong with you? It's like celebrities in New York City and Los Angeles who walk around in baseball caps and big dark glasses — the translation for which is "KEEP OUT" and also "I'm superfamous and these sunglasses cost more than your first semester in college." And meeting via the Internet — well, that was like finding your mate through the personal ads.

But my good friends Laura and Ann and I met each other through social networking about four years ago, and I now consider myself closer to them than all but a few people in my life. We'd all heard of one another before, but we'd never been in a situation to meet. (Neither of them hung out in my apartment.) Laura and I had friends in common, and Ann and I had read each other's work. But recently we admitted to feeling sheepish about this, when we were interviewing Susan Orlean, who was on our radio show while on her book tour. I'd just come back from my own book tour, and we were talking about how good it felt to go to these strange places and have Twitter or Facebook friends in the audience. There was at least one at every event of mine. Susan said she'd met several in a group for dinner. We were slightly defensive about this fact and then realized how wonderful it really had been. It reminded me of when I was traveling alone in high school (nothing exotic, I was going to Florida to visit my grandparents) and I saw Donald Sutherland in the airport. I felt a momentary rush of safe familiarity despite never having actually met him. He smiled at me and forever after I considered him a friend. (I'm sure he'd be *King of Comedy*–style thrilled to hear that.)

I noticed my connection to people online starting to change when I moved from my safe, familiar apartment to a new place. Ann and Laura were incredibly supportive. It was sixty blocks north but it felt like moving from West Germany to East Germany. The stores were unfamiliar, I missed my old neighbors, and while I was still in touch with all of my old real friends, I now had these virtual friends 24/7. You didn't have to worry about bothering them, you logged on and whoever was there was there. If you felt like joining a conversation, you could.

And if you didn't it was still a comfort to know they were available. I got a huge amount of real support from these virtual people (who actually, it turned out, were real!) and started to meet some more of them. Even if we didn't have a real person in common and all I had was a feeling about them.

Like the story of how I was born, I never tire of hearing how I became friends with someone. The thing about people you meet online is that the history of our friendship is still relatively short. So how we met is easy to remember, and also since it was fairly recent, we weren't wearing giant shoulder pads and FRANKIE SAYS RELAX T-shirts like my friends from the 1980s.

Scientists have discovered that people are attracted to mates who have complementary DNA, or opposite immune systems. They say that you can "smell" a person you are likely to successfully breed with. (There is actually a dating service that uses this now.) They also say that we are attracted to shiny hair, good teeth, bright eyes, and pretty much everything that says you're a healthy canine, too.

I think that exists in seeking platonic relationships on a different level. When I was five, I wanted to be friends with a girl on my bus named Erika Goodhart. She looked just like a doll, with pretty dark brown eyes, patent leather Mary Janes, and a bow in her hair. I knew nothing about her, except what she looked like and that her last name was the nonthreatening Goodhart. In college, I gravitated to people who wore the same punkish thrift shop clothes that I did. I don't remember smelling people but I do know that if someone smelled "bad," it wasn't necessarily a problem then.

There's a famous *New Yorker* cartoon that shows a dog sitting at the computer, telling another dog that on the Internet no one knows you're a dog. I think the same goes for whether or not you've showered or brushed your teeth or even put on pants. The "smell test" certainly wouldn't work in this case.

What you can detect is like-mindedness about politics, books, films, humor, or obsession with dogs, cats, monkeys, gourmet food, or the environment. Some people are on Twitter and Facebook simply to connect with people and raise awareness about an issue. People with similar interests or professions group up. There are mothers who blog, parents of autistic children, politicos, and foodies. I'm in a group of people who either write books or read books, but we talk about a lot of other things, too. Like whatever is in your craw that day.

I've met up with large groups of Twitter people and individually at book festivals and over lunches. I'm amazed at myself. Jancee and I used to spend hours on the phone talking about how we never wanted to meet anyone new. We were adamantly opposed to having any new friends. She would say, "Tick tock the door is locked." And I said, "No new friends unless somebody dies!" And this attitude is not uncommon. I actually have heard the Obamas instituted a "No new friends" rule in 2004 because they realized that new people might have an agenda, whereas with their old friends, they knew where they stood. Yes, I realize I have just said that Jancee and I were like the Obamas.

On the contrary, people were not banging down our doors to be our friends. We just both felt so worn out and weary of anyone new. Sometimes Jancee and I would get together over lunch at Saks, and she, who was out in the world, would meet someone new and promising. She'd serve up their dossier, relay a funny quip. We'd both be excited, and off she'd go to have dinner with them.

We'd have our postmortem and she'd say,

"Why? Why do we bother?" Of course, it turned out the person was a rabid American Girl doll collector or wanted to snort coke after coffee or, the very worst, had made dinner reservations for eight-thirty p.m. ("What is this, Spain?" Jancee would declare incredulously.)

I know that part of our dismissal of potential new pals was to relay a hidden message to each other. No one is as good as you. No one can replace you. No one will get anywhere near you in the pantheon of my friends. It was a very comforting feeling. I've watched Violet utter the magic sentence "Do you want to be my best friend?" It's good to have a wingman. Or be a wingman.

Joining the social network scene felt like a very gentle transition to meeting new people. After all, it was purportedly for work and a necessary and invaluable place for me to go. It was a great party with everyone I needed to meet, and I didn't have to get a blowout. I could just show up and chat.

Sometimes it worked in reverse. I took Violet to a colonial weathervane–making class at the Morris-Jumel Mansion museum, and there was a woman there with her daughter, whom I kept looking at because she resembled my daughter. When I called, "Violet," the other little girl turned around.

Her name was Violet, too! The coincidences were just starting. The woman and I were both born in 1966, we were both married to men named Paul. She was a writer and documentary filmmaker, and we kept saying, "I bet we know some of the same people." It was particularly striking to us because I was living in this strange neighborhood on the Harlem–Washington Heights border and I never, ever saw anyone who seemed familiar to me. Finally, the woman, Laurie, whipped out her smart phone and plugged my name into her Facebook. It showed that we had something like thirty-five friends in common. While the Violets made their weathervanes and talked about the fact that they both loved the Fairy Magic books, Laurie and I went through each person and told how we knew them.

The new friendships that I've found and strengthened on Facebook and Twitter have been wonderful, but one of the best aspects of using these services is that it allows us to reconnect with people from our past. When I signed up for Facebook I had the idea to enter the name of my first friend, Rebecca, into the search box. I hadn't seen her in thirty-some years. Though we were born in the same place, where I moved to was very different. I knew her parents had gotten divorced and her father had passed away. I wondered how all of that had affected her. I had located another acquaintance from the same era and in every picture she was holding a cigarette and a beer (but she did look happy!). She listed her nickname as "Brenda Burnout." I wondered how I'd feel if Rebecca ended up the same way.

I searched her name, and her avatar popped up. At first I thought it was a picture from when I knew her in 1969; then I realized it wasn't her. It was her daughter, who uncannily resembled her and looked about the same age as Violet. With the friend request I wrote a little note: *Wow! I can't believe I found you!* I was thrilled the next day when she accepted and wrote me a message back. She was happy to find me, too. We traded e-mails and photos and found that though our lives were different — she lived upstate in the country and I lived in the city — we had a lot more *in* common: both married with one daughter. And as our Facebook friendship developed I could see based on her posts that we agreed on politics and on what was funny, too. I was so pleased and relieved to find that she was well and happy and that she was, at least on some level, back in my life. We've still yet to meet in person again, but I know we will.

Other people I know have found old boyfriends and actually rekindled relationships. Sometimes the people I find were in my life only fleetingly but made a big impression, and being connected through Facebook feels like just the right amount of commitment.

I've heard people complain in person and in print about how social networking has caused people to be more isolated. I guess as with anything it depends on how you use it. For me, it's brought new like-minded friends into my fray and reconnected me with old friends I am sure I never would have found otherwise. And once we meet online, we are free to move things into the three-dimensional world.

CHAPTER 8
SISTERS (AND BROTHERS) FROM OTHER MOTHERS

I grew up insanely frustrated by my mother's lack of a best friend. She had friends, sure, but no one alive could touch the bond she had with her sisters Iris, Phyllis, and Mattie. So for a very long time I saw my own sisterlessness as a major deficit. How would I get through life without a sister? I begged my mother to have another daughter.

"Please, I was lucky I got you. I thought I was going to have all boys . . . like my sister."

I have two brothers, Matt and Brian. Matt is two years older than I am, and Brian is four years older. The two of them had everything in common with each other and nothing in common with me. As a child living in a rural area, I was a playdate whore, although back then they weren't called playdates; we just asked, "Can I have a friend over?" I would do everything I could to get female classmates to come over. When they arrived I'd say, "Wanna play sisters?" If they had sisters, the answer was categorically, "Noo-uhh." If they didn't, I had a sister for a few hours.

I have had the opportunity to watch my daughter go through a best friend–finding mission not unlike my own. Violet is an only child, and I know she feels a lot like I did with my two brothers. There's no one living in your house to play with. I used to make my mother play Barbies with me. She was and is a good mother, but no one alive sucked more at playing Barbies. She would just hold the doll and I'd say, "You're not doing anything!" And she'd make it hop up and down. Not fun. Nothing fun about it.

Violet was never really a Barbie fan, but she likes kids' board games. Except she cheats and makes up new rules as we're playing. Also, if it looks like I'm going to win, she tells me that I'm not being fair.

Before you're old enough to use a phone, best friends serve a different purpose. Little kids meet up in school, or they're dependent on their parents to make playdates. When Violet was little I had to go on the playdate, too. I'd make dates only with mothers I wanted to hang out with. When she was preschool age, Violet's best friends were two brothers, Aaron and Nate, because they lived a block away and their mom and I were good friends. When she started school, she had different friends every day. She has all the confidence I didn't have. I really did like almost anyone who liked me. Early on in Violet's schooling, I went by the play yard and saw her at recess. There were lots of kids playing together, but Violet was alone. The thought of her suffering like that just killed me. I walked away and sat on a bench and called my husband and, weeping, told him what I'd seen. He felt just as awful as I did about it, and I told him I'd speak to her teacher and see if there was anything to be done.

When my aunt Mattie was ten, she had two friends who ganged up on her so she had no one to eat lunch with. My grandmother sent her oldest daughter, my aunt Iris, to eat with her until the situation could be worked out. Iris was married at the time . . . and pregnant. I decided that if this kind of thing was still allowed, I would absolutely quit working to stand by my kid all day.

I made an appointment with the teacher. She knew all about it. "It isn't that no one wants to play with Violet," she said reassuringly. "She doesn't want to play with anyone who won't play the game she makes up, so she'd rather play alone." In fact, Violet was fine. The following year she found a slightly more compliant group of friends, and now she understands that you need to have give-and-take in your friend-ships . . . until you become a greedy CEO, and then you can go back to making every-one do what you want.

When I was in junior high, my best friends were anyone I could find who would en-hance my potential for acceptance. I'd look for someone who dressed perfectly or did really well in school to offset my not having those qualities. Proximity always played heavily into it. Like the first friend I had who lived on my small dead-end street, it was most convenient to have a best friend within walking distance, even though in Ka-tonah it was more like agonizing, wheezy, sweaty hiking distance.

By high school I realized I was a bit dif-ferent from everyone else. You see, I found out that simply by thinking it, I could make myself fly. Not really, but everyone thinks they have realized that they're different from everyone else in high school. Some people squash the feelings into a cheerleading uniform or with a science award, and others wear black nail polish and listen to the Dead Boys. I was the latter, because I had to be. I was utterly and completely unathletic to the point of being at the least a detriment and at most a danger to any team I might actually make, but I did find a place to belong among the music and theater kids. It was then I decided that I was going to be an actress when I grew up. I remember telling my grandparents when I was in Florida visiting them for midwinter vacation. My grandmother said to me, "How can you be an actress? You're too fat!" And my grandfather said, "She can be an actress. Look at Colleen Dewhurst!" He was defending me . . . sort of. You know that whole thing about grandparents and unconditional love? Me neither.

I was so happy to have made new friends who embraced my lack of coordination with a field hockey stick. None of them could catch a ball either, and when they tried to jump over a hurdle, it all came tumbling down. My new group of close friends was a happy, safe place where having awful grades and no letter jacket was your ticket in. The leader of the "Drammies" was a teacher named Gilbert Freeman, who lived in New York City and commuted to our high school. He was beyond the coolest of the cool in our view, and he accepted us. He ran the music and theater departments and was the director of the choir, the annual variety show, and the plays. We didn't audition for choir; if you wanted to be in it, you could be. It was just a group of kids who spent their days not playing outside but inside reading books or watching movies — my people. There was such a beauty to being a part of that group that I had a hard time finding it again in college. I still count a few of the Drammies among my closest friends.

It turned out that I wasn't really cut out to be an actor, so I pursued film, but I realized I wasn't really crazy about film, either. I liked watching movies, but I wasn't so sure I wanted to make them. Most of the other film students walked around with light meters hanging from their necks and lenses in their pocket. I made one good friend in film school, Vesna, because we both agreed we didn't want to be filming at one in the morning. We wanted to be sleeping. We built a friendship on a similar aspiration to slack. In the end, it turned out she was no slacker; after college she did premed and eventually became a doctor. I'm still friends with her despite that gross misrepresentation.

After college, many friends came in the form of coworkers. But those relationships mostly ended when the jobs did, while friendships of more serendipitous origins persisted. Jancee and I became friends after a chance meeting on an uncomfortable hayride magically turned us into best friends. Barbara and I met in fifth grade; we were both dorks and that keeps us close even today. My friend Deb and I met at a book event when her father had just been diagnosed with cancer and I offered to take care of her dog when she went out of town. My friend Patty and I met at our agent's mother's funeral. And of course Ann and Laura and I met through social networking. There's not really a formula for where or when to find a friend, but at this point in my life, I can tell pretty quickly if someone is going to be in my life for a while.

Our lives have gotten so busy that there is barely time for the people who feel vital, but I believe very strongly in holding onto close friends. There are times when I realize that a person I used to talk to five times a day has been relegated to annual catch-up status, and it saddens me that I no longer have any idea what they like to eat for lunch. But I still think about them all the time. My friends are my fortune, and I try to let them know when they've popped into my head, even if it's because the store where we knocked over a giant glass bottle of pickled eggs has closed.

Feeling so strongly about my close friends was one of the reasons I felt comfortable having only one child. Having an only child was something I never expected. I always wondered if I'd have three or four and then maybe only two, but I never thought I'd have just one. It seemed so sad and solitary to have no siblings. I pictured the only child wearing a backward baseball cap, tossing a ball against the wall of the tenement, a rat his only confidant. I can recall knowing just one only child from my elementary school days. She was the daughter of two older professors, a brainy girl who read constantly and sucked her thumb for way too long and then graduated from high school two years early. Not a great track record. There were a few kids in my kindergarten class who had brothers and sisters in college and they kind of seemed like only children, but they weren't. My father's mother was told she couldn't have any kids at all, because at age twelve, in 1913, she was run over by a truck and her back was broken. My father's birth was nothing short of a miracle, only to be outdone when he was fifteen by the arrival of his baby sister, Susie. The bulk of his early life was spent alone; both of his parents worked. By the time Susie came along, he was about ready to go to college. They certainly were never playmates. His stories of being a boy are about the saddest and loneliest you could ever imagine. Why would anyone do that to a kid if they didn't have to?

I didn't get married until I was thirty-five, and by that time I was already on the oldish side for having kids. I got pregnant a couple of months after the wedding and had a pretty dreadful and dangerous pregnancy, and gave birth prematurely. My husband and I celebrated our first anniversary in the maternity ward with our tiny little girl hooked up to a dozen wires and monitors. It took me longer than I'd hoped to recover, and by that point we were experiencing severe financial woes. At the right time biologically to conceive again, it just seemed like the worst idea possible. What if I had another difficult pregnancy? I had been on bed rest last time; how could I possibly do that with a little toddler running around? I know people do it, and my sister-in-law had to, but it wasn't something I felt like I could manage. I thought maybe at some point we'd think about adopting, but mainly I was just trying to make things work with what we had. Every so often I'd debate the topic with my husband, and then I'd feel horribly guilty for not wanting to go through another pregnancy. We had chosen to live in Manhattan, where everything cost more, space was harder to come by, and getting into a good public school was a big honking deal. It wasn't an easy proposition in the best of situations.

I stopped feeling guilty only when Violet started school and her class was about fifty percent single children (the other half were twins!). It turned out not to be such an oddity. She was friends with her classmates, we got together with them outside school, and she was alone just when she wanted to be — certainly less than I had been growing up with brothers. Also, apartment living is much less solitary than growing up rural. I do adore my brothers and am thrilled that they have kids so that my daughter can be close to her cousins. I am confident that when the time arrives in Violet's life for her to need the support of someone, she'll have a mate or friends who will be there for her.

My mother's relationships with her sisters certainly served as a role model for me with my friendships. I knew there was something she got from them that she didn't get from anyone else. Now I see how Violet watches me with my friends. When she was a toddler, she'd pretend to be on the phone with

Jancee and she'd do this fake doubled-over laughing thing, and she'd mumble conspiratorially into her phone. She knows how important it is for me to see my friends alone and that there is something special about making time for those people, that they "feed" me. I've watched her develop into such a sweet friend to her own friends, looking for ways to make them feel good. Worrying about them when they seem sad. I am so proud of the friend she is. There is nothing I would rather pass on to her from me . . . other than possibly a signature dance move or two.

CHAPTER 9
THE CALL OF DUTY

I had two near-death experiences in a single night because I answered the call of friendship. I wish I could say I had sacrificed myself for a friend in the trenches at Verdun, but I was just in a rock club with my old college friend Katie. She had a crush on a hardcore punk singer and made me go to his shows with her. Never has there been a more reluctant denizen of the mosh pit. I believe I was the only one in there yelling, "Ow! Quit it!" Anyway, I was standing in the pit when a shirtless guy landed on my head. Near-death experience number one was that he almost flattened me. Near-death experience number two was that his sweaty chest touched my face and I'm pretty sure he was the last known carrier of bubonic plague.

It's rarely that dramatic, but frequently it's necessary as a friend to come to the aid of a lovelorn lass or lad who needs you to make them feel less stupid standing in the hall outside biology or waiting all day in Starbucks for a heavily strategized chance meeting. You think this happens only in high school and college, but I'm here to tell you I've done this through my thirties. I actually dragged my friend Barbara to a course in biodiversity at the American Museum of Natural History so she could sit with me while I watched the dreamy scientist talk about our vanishing ecosystems. I should say that at no time was her life in any danger unless you believe that a person really can be bored to death.

Most of the things we do for friends fall into the category of mildly uncomfortable, but as loyal troopers we suck it up and do them anyway. In my case, I like to go to bed at nine-thirty p.m., so when anyone asks me to do anything that goes later than that, I consider it a huge sacrifice.

In fact, I think eighty-five percent of the things I do for a friend that I don't want to do but have to involve my staying up late. Or going to Brooklyn. The other fifteen percent is made up of equal parts waiting for someone's cable to be installed and being a bridesmaid, though for only one of my times as a bridesmaid was my dress so ugly I "accidentally" threw it away after the wedding. Then there are the things we don't want to do because they're painful to our friends, like seeing a divorce attorney with them or going to a scary doctor's appointment. These things might fall at inconvenient times, but you realize immediately how important your presence and support is for your friend. That's when you bite the bullet, put your head down, and do it, and realize it ain't about you.

About four years ago, a close friend of mine was trying to lose weight. It had been a real struggle for her for a long time, and she finally wanted to get control over it. She is a beautiful woman and I always thought of her as voluptuous, with a Marilyn Monroe type of body. But we all have our own comfort zones, or what we think are our comfort zones. I had issues with weight in college, brought on by ordering in hot fudge sundaes and deciding to be a vegetarian, except that instead of vegetables I ate just macaroni and cheese with a side of fries. I gained a lot of weight, but I really ate good stuff (I mean good-tasty, not good for you). I had a little group of dorm friends, none of whom had a boyfriend other than Bob of Bob's Big Boy or the guy who delivered our Swensen's ice cream.

After college I worked at a weight-loss

center and started learning something about why people gain weight and have trouble losing it, and having successfully lost the fifty pounds I gained in college made me kind of an expert about weight loss with my friends. I'd often get asked for help, and I was happy to provide it, so when my friend asked me to help her with her goal, I was completely on board.

I took walks with her and she checked in with me about her exercise routines, and she'd tell me how her eating was going. I asked her why she wanted me to do it when there was a world of professionals out there who probably had piles of handy printouts. She said they didn't love her and so would be less invested in her success, and she wanted to be able to call me about it anytime. Also, she pointed out, I didn't cost her anything.

So we set off on our little plan. Every night she'd check in with me, like a sponsor, and we'd chat about what happened during her day. If she ate more than she intended to at an office birthday party, we talked about ways she might be able to avoid it in the future. If she slept through her alarm and didn't make it to the gym, we talked about why that might have happened and I would remind her that you need decent sleep to lose weight, too. I felt good about helping her, she was making progress on her weight-loss plan, and for the first time in our friendship we were not letting weeks go by without a phone call or an in-person visit.

About two months into it, we were having a long chat on the phone and she confessed to me that she'd stopped dieting and going to the gym. Work had gotten crazy and she just wasn't that into trying to lose weight anymore. She realized it was better for her to get off the plan than to feel like she was failing every day. We were both kind of quiet. I said there was no reason we couldn't still keep talking, but our daily conversations didn't really last. We went back to our old ways of checking in every now and then, and it was a bit sad.

It made me realize how much being asked for help can aid a friendship. The friend who asks for help and receives it feels nurtured and cared for, and giving the help makes you feel needed and important. Though it's temporary, it can be a huge nurturing boost to the relationship.

A couple of years ago I had to make a short movie for a book. I was very anxious about it; I just couldn't see how it was going to work. My friend Ann had been making these little funny videos and posting them on her blog. Some were quite complicated, most involved her motley crew of animals as actors. Seeing her talent and interest, I asked her if maybe she'd want to help me with my project. She leaped at the chance, closet Cecil B. DeMille that she was. We started discussing it in May and decided we'd film it in June. Her son was in film school, so he could shoot it for us. Then he'd edit it and we'd have a fine little film.

We had our date and did our shoot and realized we did not have enough material. By not enough I mean nothing. Essentially we were making a film out of our heads — no script or storyboard, just some funny ideas or what we thought were funny ideas. As proof, if you watch the video you can hear Ann cracking up in the background. Once we watched the footage, we realized we were going to have to do more filming. Unfortunately, Ann's film school–educated son had a job, and as much as he wanted to hang out with his mom and her middle-aged friend who didn't have any idea what they were doing, he really couldn't.

So Ann took up the mantle and became a producer/director/friend indeed. Our little book video went from being a two-week project to taking close to three months. Ann filmed me on several occasions and in various locations, and she booked us stellar guest stars. She bought an expensive film editing program and taught herself how to cut a short film, including sound and music editing.

It turned into one of the highlights of what had been a very tough year for me. We both had a blast doing it and whenever we panicked about it actually sucking, we remembered that it was a book trailer. Who the hell even knew what they were, let alone watched them? When it was all done, I was relieved that Ann's wonderful gesture had finally concluded and she could get back to her own busy life — but I also felt a bit bereft. Ann and I had had reason to talk on the phone several times a day for months, and now we were done.

The whole time she never complained. I'd call her and say, "Be honest, you'd like to roll back the tape to when you said, 'Sure, I'd love to.' "

"Not at all!" she'd say. "I'm having fun. I love learning new things. I think this is really good for me!"

So not only had she helped me out enormously, beyond what I could even say here, she did it gladly. And coming to people's aid without making them feel guilty is key. I know this because when I've been in the position to help someone, I'm so busy telling them what a great friend I am and how lucky they are to have me, who is so willing and exuberant, that I believe it almost erases the gesture.

I used to listen to a long-standing fight between some roommates I was friends with. One said if you were asked to do a favor and actually did it, that was what counted, not the manner in which it was done. The other said if you did it half-assed or grumpily or late, it didn't count. I think I agree with both of them. If I am donating a kidney to a friend and decide to do so of my own free will, I'd better do so without grumbling, lest I make my sick friend feel guilty and awful. But if you are going to ask me to move a couch up seven flights of stairs, I'm allowed to complain, even if you buy me a pizza and some beer. Complaining is kind of my way of communicating, but I hope to do it in an entertaining way. I'll check with my friends and see if I accomplish that. It was actually Violet who pointed out to me that when I do something nice, she knows she's going to have to hear about it for a whole year. Thank God for the honesty of our children.

Being a parent has introduced me to so

many wonderful things, but kids' birthday parties do not rank among them. They remind me of being sober at a frat party. All those tiny pieces of cold pizza, the games that everyone has to win, kids so sugared up they could almost take flight. Not only are they the height of not fun, they're smack dab in the middle of a weekend day. Yet when it's your own kid, attendance is unavoidable, unless you want to be the subject of several future therapy sessions. When it's someone else's kid, well, attendance is second only to martyrdom.

I often invite my friends without kids to Violet's parties in the hopes that we can steal a few minutes to chat. And truthfully, her parties are usually better than most because she insists on having them on her actual birthday, which frequently falls on Labor Day weekend when no one is around so it's just us and a lot of cupcakes. For Violet's eighth birthday, she wanted a karaoke party. We found a place in downtown Manhattan and she invited ten of her closest friends. We brought sparkly hats and crowns, boas, and sunglasses. There were chicken wings, those tiny cold slices of pizza, and some Thai appetizers. We also brought in a few bowls of chips and pretzels and M&M's. The floor was slick with spills and the streamers and balloons we had put up fell down and were sailing through the murky swamp. If that wasn't appealing enough, the girls were singing along to Taio Cruz, Katy Perry, Lady Gaga, and the Ke$ha song where she brushes her teeth with a bottle of Jack. These girls didn't know from ballads.

Across the room on a bench sat Barbara and my friend Brenda with smiles plastered on their faces. Because of the way the RSVPs came in, I had been worried that there wouldn't be enough kids, so Barbara and Brenda came to fill in. Violet told her friends that Barbara and Brenda (both in their mid-forties) were "teenagers," and she said so with conviction, so they weren't getting nothing for their troubles! I looked at them jovial and participatory, complimenting the singers on their vocal prowess. And suddenly I was overcome with guilt. These were two very busy professionals who worked long hours during the week and used the weekends to catch up on everything from laundry to exercise to just a moment of peace, and I had commandeered two of their precious Saturday hours and asked them to sit in this sticky, loud jungle. I walked over to them and sat down between them and as audibly as I could, said, "I'm so sorry." They both laughed. Barbara said she was going to do a song soon and Brenda just kept politely saying, "I've never seen anything like it." They were sweet and gracious as could be, never once trying to choke me or tie the Monster High napkins together to escape out the window. I really was so happy to have them there, they made the day infinitely better for me and Violet. I'd like to say that I won't make them do it again next year, but I'm afraid that's simply not true.

In the past, women of a certain station in life had one person they always knew would meet the call of duty, and she was referred to as a lady-in-waiting. She would either be compensated or not, and in a sense her role was like that of a mandatory friend. The lady-in-waiting couldn't say, "Oh no, Marie Antoinette, I'm not going to back up your iPod, I've got a Pilates class." She had to or she'd have to eat cake with no head, which I think was the going punishment at the time. The duties of ladies-in-waiting varied from court to court but included such tasks as: knowing proper etiquette, having proficiency in languages and dance steps, performing secretarial tasks, reading aloud, writing correspondence, sewing, painting, horseback riding, music making (singing or maybe playing the lute), as well as advising and taking care of wardrobe, supervising servants, keeping the lady in tune with gossip and current palace affairs, and, as I've gathered from several period films, putting secret messages into her cleavage.

Today you probably don't have a lady-in-waiting, unless you're Kate Middleton, but you may have had a wedding with bridesmaids who sort of operated like modern ladies-in-waiting. Depending on the bride, that is.

An old friend of mine from college brilliantly tells the story of a bride she "attended." The woman was from a family that had once been loaded — the kind that had debutante balls and butlers — but all the money had been lost by an uncle who was the drunken, debauching, Monaco-hopping philanderer of the family. I always imagined him as a sort of cross between Steve McQueen and Anthony Newley with a little Linus Larrabee thrown in. Anyway, the parents were decent, but the children, including the daughter my friend was friends with, were nightmares. They were continually railing about the unfair loss of their estate. To no one's surprise, the daughter found someone who could ease her financial pain, and they were to be married. According to my friend, she balled up all the years of raging self-pity she could muster and hurled it at her bridesmaids like a spiked flail.

I know this so-called "Bridezilla" phenomenon has been well documented in magazine articles and reality TV shows, and I think because of that, it seems that a certain segment of the population feels that it's acceptable to be insufferable.

No matter what you may have heard or seen, it is not.

I'm not a psychologist or a life coach, but I am going to throw down the gauntlet here and say no one should be a Bridezilla anymore. It is unforgivable to ever treat your friends poorly, but it is especially unconscionable to do it when you're asking them to stand up for you. As it is, you're already expecting them to travel to wherever you've decided to get married, buy some dress that no matter how much you think they'll be able to wear it again, they will not, do their hair in ringlets, dance with your cousin Vito. It really is a day to be grateful that so many people are coming together to support you.

Whether slam dancing in the mosh pit or walking down the aisle, close friendships always require sacrifices. Some are small, and some are larger. That is the nature of life, but it is never an excuse for intentional cruelty. In fact, the times I've been able to sacrifice for a friend, or had a friend step in for me, have led to some of my greatest discoveries about the depth and strength of my friendships. I don't know that I would have found them otherwise. Bonds are forged and certainly strengthened during rough times.

I remember when I took care of my friend Deb's dog when her father was very ill. When she came to pick up the dog she said to me, "Your karma is so good now, you're going to have massages and hot fudge sundaes every day in heaven."

I held her hands and said, "Being able to help you is the reward . . . and also, um, I don't really want to be dead."

CHAPTER 10
DON'T BE A DRAIN

A college roommate of mine used to call her best friend from high school every Sunday. I would be on my bed studying . . . a takeout menu, and she'd be sitting at her desk. I'd listen to the progression of the call. It would begin with a perky "Hi!" and then continue into a long silence broken up by an occasional sympathetic noise. After a few minutes, I would see my roommate's shoulders sinking, her face falling, and her pen doodling. By the end of the forty-five minutes to an hour she would spend on the phone, she'd be slumped down like a beaten-up pair of acid-washed jeans. They'd say their good-byes and my roommate would hang up the phone, lie down on her bed, and fall into a deep sleep. Week after week I'd watch this routine, until the very mention of my roommate's best friend's name at any time or place would have me yawning, barely able to keep my eyes open.

I was taking Psych 101 at the time, and we were studying abusive relationships. It occurred to me that this friendship of my roommate's was kind of like that! My room-mate wasn't an insomniac, so being put to sleep was not helpful, and other than a sleep aid, I couldn't see her getting anything out of the relationship. I decided to broach the subject with her over French fries and macaroni and cheese in the dining hall.

"Have you ever thought that maybe you were in an unhealthy relationship?" I asked, clinically.

"I don't even have a boyfriend!" she said.

Ah, I thought, these mental novices, the poor lost people who haven't taken three weeks of Introduction to Psychology. I explained to her that I meant that her conversations with her best friend literally enervated her right before my eyes every week. She listened politely, as we know she was very capable of doing, and then told me I was way off base. From then on I just went to the dorm lounge when she made her calls and minded my own business.

My college roommate aside, I think it's fair to say that unless you look like Robert Pattinson, nobody wants you sucking the life out of them. Everyone experiences times in

153

their life when they need a lot of support, and that's okay. If a close family member becomes ill or your long-term relationship is breaking up, you should have a good network of friends that you can call upon at any time of the day or night when you need someone to listen. Sometimes the burden falls mostly on one friend, and that's just how it is, but that is why we should take good care of our friendships, because at those hopefully rare times in our life when we need nourishing, we should have a harvest to draw from.

Now, notice I was very specific about the two (2) to three (3) potential situations that qualify as a crisis that entitles you to lean on your friends harder than usual. Becoming ill, getting divorced, or having a sick child, parent, or spouse qualify, but there is a big difference between a crisis and a chronic situation. There aren't *really* only two or three acceptable crises, there are as many as there are types of parasites that can attach themselves to your organs and rob you of vital nutrients. But your crisis needs to meet certain criteria in your situation in order to justify bugging your friends, and you need to take steps to solve it, if applicable. If you're a farmer on an island off Benarobia, and your goat is depressed, that might be a time when you need to call the Elders in for a rap session. If you live in Manhattan and your goat is depressed, you should bring him to a psychoanalyst and not be bothering anyone else.

Throughout the history of friendship there have been these people: relationship remoras. Do you know what I mean? Remoras are fish whose bellies are "suckers." Their lives consist of attaching to the back of a host — a shark, whale, turtle, dugong — and living off it. When the whale eats a huge mouthful of krill, the ones that he lets go get eaten by the remora, or when the whale eats a mouthful of krill and takes a big whale of a dump, the remora eats that. Some remoras live in the mouths of fish. Can you imagine how annoying that would be? You can just picture the poor tuna and swordfish thinking they ate a bad clam, but really it's a flippin' remora!

Some remora and host pairings provide mutual benefits. The remora cleans bacteria off the shark or whale or turtle in exchange for the free room and board. Still, it's not like the remora has been invited. The turtle doesn't put an ad in the *Undersea Gazette* and then interview a bunch of remoras to decide whom they want to be stuck to. The remora just sees an opening and sticks its sucky self right in.

If you're like me, even the word "remora" conjures the face of an old friend and makes you shudder. Haven't we all had the experience of being a host to an unwanted drain? That person who just catches a ride and takes and takes and takes from you.

You wonder how anyone would get into this mess of a pseudo-friendship. I found myself vulnerable to soul-sucking at points in my life when I was more . . . how do you say, desperate. I met one of these people in a bar I had gone to with a bunch of friends. She was pretty and fun and wore really cool clothes. The boys were drawn to her and she liked me. She pressed me to leave and go to another and then another and then another bar with her. I obliged, and then bleary eyed at the end of the way-too-late-for-me night, I gave her my number.

We were friends for one season, from January to April. It was a time in my life when I could illustrate myself as a coat rack, just there to throw your jacket over. I never stood up for myself. During the day we'd have multi-hour phone calls, discussing how her night had gone, the men who adored her, what she wore and what she would wear the next night, and if she should wear her hair up or down. Then she'd break it up by telling me about her crazy childhood in India and Africa and New York. Her parents were divorced, her mother dated famous rock stars, and her dad was a plastic surgeon who had apparently done the tits of "everyone in the seventies." I was dazzled by her for a couple of weeks, but then I just got so, so tired. I didn't want to pick up the phone when she called, I didn't want to think about her, and I didn't want to go on the forced march that was our nights of gallivanting. Yet when I'd say "no thanks" she'd boost me with a couple of well-placed compliments, like a boxer's coach slitting open his swollen eye, and I'd end up saying yes.

People can seem like a lot of fun initially, and only when you've found yourself compromising in too many ways do you realize they're remoras. This is where knowing the difference between chronic and crisis is important. Do you know anyone who cancels plans only with great drama? It's never "You know, I had a long week and it's raining and I just don't want to go out." It's "My uncle, who just suffered the loss of his wife, had terrible stomach pains and we thought it was appendicitis. I was the only one who could take him to the emergency room and it took him hours to get a bed. Right now I'm waiting for his son to get here from Chapel Hill, North Carolina, and . . ." By the time the story is done, you've finished the crossword and moved on. You've been put in a place where not only can't you be disappointed that your plans have been canceled, you're also being forced to comfort the friend. People who are going through something genuinely difficult deserve comfort. Sometimes it seems like one thing after another because it really is. But when you just know someone has come up with a wild story to get out of a plan, you are possibly being gamed by a friendship remora. Their story may have at one point had a grain of truth. The uncle had suffered the loss of his wife . . . in the Paramus mall . . . but then he found her at Cinnabon.

I have a hard time asking anyone for help with my problems. I will tell my friends about something when it's all been solved. It's something I've worked on over the years, but I still feel deep down like I should be able to take care of myself and not pester anyone. "Do you need anything?" I'm asked. "No thanks, I'm fine," I reply, hooked up to an IV for dehydration.

I grew up privileged with stuff, and in

many ways I still feel like that, though now it's actually the things that money can't buy that make me feel lucky. I've also had streaks of incredibly bad luck. One streak lasted for seven years. I kept looking for shards of a broken mirror. During that period, I talked to friends, but not more than I felt was fair. I asked a few friends recently if they remember my lengthy stretch of bad luck and if they dreaded hearing from me then. No one recalled me complaining a lot, but two friends said that whenever we got together I just sat with eyebrows furrowed, breathing shallowly. They did say they would have preferred if I had shared my woes. I guess part of me still thinks when I'm having a problem that there's nothing that talking about it can do to help. If I need a job and you don't have one for me, what good is telling you going to do? Can you make me pregnant? Can you make thirty-five thousand dollars magically appear in my bank account? No? Then why talk about it?

But the truth is, talking about stuff helps. Talking allows you to find out that you aren't alone, and can provide insight into how someone else coped with what you're experiencing. Just hearing your own words outside of your head can help. I've had friends struggle with one particular issue for years — not being able to meet the right guy, battling body issues — and because they are trying to make changes and willing to work on it, I'm always happy to hear about it. But part of the reason I like to listen is that now I force myself (and I do mean force) to share back. It really doesn't work if only one of you is divulging struggles, except in very special cases, when that's the only way it will work. When a friend's mother was diagnosed with stage 4 leukemia, it wasn't my time to share. It was my turn to listen and do whatever I could to ease her pain.

If you feel like you're being depleted by a friendship, it's important to try to talk about it. You need to be able to tell the difference between a remora and a true friend who is just having issues. Tell them how you feel, don't recount to them what they're doing. If a friend feels that they really need all that time and help on a regular basis, they should be seeking some kind of professional counsel and you might be the best person to persuade them to start getting help from somewhere else. Remember: Give a man a fish, feed him for day; teach a man to go to therapy, get him to stop hitching rides on the backs of sharks.

160

CHAPTER 11
RULES OF WAR

I'm happy to say I've had only one friendship ever break up. It happened when my best friend Barbara and I were living together in our sophomore year of college. Barbara's sister Kristin, who was a year younger than us, was our other best friend, and I always said to them if either of them had the choice to save me or one of them from a burning building, they'd choose each other. Because, you know, blood is thick and all. I believe it was a confluence of things that caused the breakup. In some way we must have needed to be apart from each other to change and grow up; after all, we'd been best friends since fifth grade. Barbara was in art school and I was at NYU, and she began going to parties and bars and out with guys, and I was still renting movies and eating pizza. I wanted us to stay where we were, and she was ready to branch out.

As I predicted, when Barbara and I had

our falling-out, Kristin sided with Barbara. I can't even remember what the actual fight that sparked our breakup was about. I don't believe Kristin really had a choice. It was a bad, weird, horrible time. We had gone from the three of us doing everything together to me on my own.

Kids today learn to express every nuance of feeling that creeps into their constellation. My daughter has told me that I've hurt her socks' feelings, and yes, I apologized. Every school year starts with a list of classroom rules that emphasize kindness and respect, so that students learn to disagree peaceably and can follow cues to figure out when to cooperate and when to stand up for themselves. In pre-K and kindergarten, the list of rules in Violet's classroom included:

- Always say "sure" if someone wants to play.

- You can say "no" if you don't want to play.

- No tea parties in the bathroom.

- Don't pick your nose.

- Private parts are private.

- Please don't throw things at people.

- Never, ever touch anyone or scare them unless they say it's okay.

- Say nice words to everyone and don't tell anyone they're stupid.

- No being tough to anyone.

- No saying bathroom words except in the bathroom.

- Don't laugh at anyone who's not trying to be funny.

- No hitting, no pushing, no biting, no pulling hair, no pulling people, no punching, no kicking, no poking, no biting anyone [again].

- Don't say, "You can't sit at this table," "You can't sit next to me."

- Keep this a happy room.

It's a different time now, but this chapter is for people who come from my planet, which is still stuck somewhere in the 1970s, not this new expressive one. It took me a good long while to realize that you could have a disagreement with a friend and they wouldn't necessarily explode or kill you, or more likely, dissolve the friendship. Over time I learned that what actually weakens a friendship is when one party (me, in this case) doesn't express their negative feelings. Before learning this, I had ended up killing off relationships because I was so angry at my friends for not "letting me" say how I felt.

My parents didn't fight when I was a kid. My father would say something to piss off my mother, she would give him the silent treatment for a week, and then sometime somewhere that I wasn't, they'd eventually work it out, or she'd forget it. She grew up the same way I did, without learning tools for fixing interpersonal problems. Today, Violet and her friends are trained in "mediation" techniques, and when they reach fifth grade, they patrol the playground at recess helping the younger kids sort out fights and negotiate solutions. It's positively futuristic!

Through volunteering at the playground I realized that many of these kids would grow up without the hang-ups of my generation and, in fact, ruin society by putting all the people in the psychotherapy/divorce professions right out of business. In the meantime, I'd watch them and learn.

When you have no experience working through anger, it's an incredibly frightening feeling. I spent a good portion of my early life honing my skills in conflict avoidance, staying out of not only my own conflicts but those around me. If I saw people's not-so-nice feelings brewing, I'd diffuse them with a joke or a compliment or pretend I was having a heart attack. It was so effective that I actually thought I was a great friend, but in fact I was a terrible friend and not so healthy either.

There was a time when you could not drag the bad feelings out of me. Now I force people to tell me that I made them mad. Really, I say, I can take it, I understand. One of the most important lessons I've learned in my life is to look at where someone is coming from and understand that you mostly won't know. You don't get a person's biography when they're waiting on you in a restaurant or even teaching your child. I have a busy life in a hectic city, and I ain't Mother Teresa or Gandhi — or Freud, for that matter. My frequent reaction to a person who is rude to me is to be rude back. I was recently at the gym and one of the three StairMasters was broken. A guy was using one and I was using the other. A woman in the gym whom I had always hated came up to me and told me I had to get off after thirty minutes because that was the rule when someone was waiting. Let me first explain why I hated her: (1) she does push-ups in the walkway where people are trying to walk; (2) she uses hand weights on the StairMaster and leaves them there; (3) she is impolite and argumentative. So I had already had this reaction to her and now she was trying to cut into my already tight workout time. I was getting ready to lay into her when the man across from me, a guy who always has a smile on his face, said, "I'm done. You can use this one." And then when she got over there, he cleaned it off, looked her in the face, and said, "Have a great day." I watched him in abject horror, and then he turned to me and gave me a conspiratorial wink and smile. "Have a great day," I said to him. The woman said nothing to either of us. She was too busy doing pull-ups on the side bars, exercising, exercising, like some kind of possessed demon! After he walked away, I had this fantasy where she would tell me to get off the machine and I'd turn it off and apologize, saying, "I'm sorry I was hogging the machine. A workout is the only time I feel good because my best friend is DYING OF CANCER IN A HOSPICE!" Then, THEN, she'd feel guilty for pushing me out of my one small bright spot of my really sad day.

And then I thought, What if her best friend is dying of cancer in a hospice and that's why she's so nuts. Or maybe she has a drug-addicted daughter or her husband just left her for a twenty-three-year-old bikini model. Looking at someone in that way changes everything. It can help you see the other person as a human being, even if you might disagree with them about something.

With our friends, we do know their biographies and sometimes that gets in the way. I am now a person who embraces confrontation. I'm no longer afraid because I know I'm good at working through to the other side. Sometimes, though, my knowledge of a person's baggage prevents me from expressing my feelings, because I know they were abandoned by their mother or abused by their boyfriend and I measure their responses by where I know they are coming from. I used to get angry at a friend who was always late, and I'd never express it. I'd think, Oh, I know she's always late because her mother used to set her alarm for four a.m. . . . So I would just sit on my feelings and be understanding on the outside, while stewing in resentment on the inside. Now I know that the way I find myself "protecting" friends is really quite damaging to us both. What is much healthier is to say, "I know you have trouble being on time, but it makes me feel like you don't consider me important enough to make the effort for." That way you've given your friend a chance to see how their actions affect the world around them, and you've shown them you have faith that they care about you and, in this case, can do better.

My mother tried very hard to protect me from any discomfort in my childhood. If things felt too hard for me, she'd let me quit. I faulted her for that until I became a parent, when I learned that it is true when they say, "Wait'll you have your own kids." I find the most difficult part of parenting is helping my daughter negotiate difficulty by not getting her out of it. One year she started school with a known "bad teacher." A mother at drop-off asked me if I was going to pull her out of the school. I guess if you didn't grow up the way I did, that idea wouldn't sound the way I heard it — like extreme child abuse. The fact is the world has many more people who don't dance you around on a chair and totally get you and give you special treatment than those who do. In my mind, the earlier you learn to be around that vast majority of people, the better. It's the same with friends. You are much more helpful to them if you share the way things they do make you feel than if you ignore it and let them go out into the world and do it to everyone else.

Has anyone ever asked you, "Why didn't you tell me I was being such a bitch?" A friend of mine once did. She had been going through a very hard time, getting married to someone in Australia with a lot of family *mishegoss.* I didn't tell her because, well, I understood it. She was actually quite angry with me, saying, "I count on you to be honest with me. I was nasty to everyone and you didn't tell me!"

We're all different, and our styles are different, but hopefully the friends who are close to you can manage your feelings. You shouldn't be having *a lot* of arguments with your close friends unless you're thirteen. As adultish-type people, we mostly don't fight. I can think of maybe three fights I've had with my best friends in the last ten years. Partly it's because I've culled the people who cause me too much grief and partly because we're all so old that we are much less sensitive. I assume when someone tells me that I've done something to make them angry it was because I had my head up my butt with my own life. I always listen very carefully to what happened and try to figure out where I was and what was going on with me at the time that could have led to my insensitive behavior. After I give them my list of excuses for why I did what I did, which was totally my fault, I apologize.

Ann and Laura and I do a radio show together. Ann is Irish Catholic and Laura is Jewish Neurotic. Laura and I have similar tendencies, as I am also JN. There was a time when I hadn't really heard from Ann for a while, other than a single quick e-mail. It was before we started doing the show together, so we weren't as clued in to each other's schedules. I carefully combed through the conversations I'd had with Ann before she disappeared, picking out a few possible reasons that I could have made her mad and sent her packing. Most likely, I reasoned, she was done being my friend and would never speak to me again because of my blatant insensitivity. I actually considered deleting her from my contact list because it was so painful to remember the good friend I once had who was no longer there. About a week into my mourning, I contacted Laura and asked her if she knew why Ann hated my guts now. I learned that I was wrong; apparently, it was Laura who drove Ann away and had done it in such a way that Ann had probably dropped me as a friend because she was now totally turned off to Jews. How had Laura managed this? She wasn't sure, she knew only that it was she and her thoughtless cloddishness that did it. We went back and forth and then wondered, Maybe, maybe it had nothing to do with us. Maybe, just maybe, it wasn't all about us. As preposterous as this sounded, we considered it, neither of us convinced. We'd check in about it from time to time, and then we got an e-mail from Ann. She'd been away with her family on an island without Internet or cell phone service. It was a last-minute thing and we weren't besties at that time so she didn't think to tell us. Laura and I laughed and laughed. We laughed the laugh of the stupid narcissist. *It had nothing to do with us. Things happen in the world that we don't cause.*

We all learned something: Laura and I to take a deep breath, and Ann that when she is going away she needs to send an itinerary to us and maybe draw little hearts all over it so we know she hasn't left town because she hates us.

What's the lesson in this? Before you make an assumption, check it out. Before you decide someone is not speaking to you because you defied them and bought that fuchsia muumuu, check in with them. If they don't answer, don't assume they are dead or hate you; those things are most unlikely. And if you are friends with people and you are going through something that's keeping you from regular communications, let them know. There are times, though, that we are dealing with stresses in our lives that make it hard to have regular contact. Sometimes it's job difficulty, sometimes it's money, or a new baby or a sick kid or sick parent or sick dog, and it's all you can do to hold it together for yourself. You just can't make small talk and maybe you don't want to big talk. Maybe you just want to sink into a book. But it's a good idea to let the people who think about you know where you're at. Because it's not a nice feeling to wonder if someone has ditched you, and you also might be surprised at the comfort a friend can give you even in a brief exchange.

You want your friendships to be as healthy as they can be, and the only way to do that is to bring your feelings, good or bad, out into the open. It's important to fight, but if

172

you find yourself only fighting, then maybe the friendship has run its course. And also know that it's okay sometimes to just let something go.

In our younger days, Barbara and I would fight, and it would culminate in our not speaking for days. It was in the midst of one of these vows of silence that we each found ourselves looking for a taxi in the snow at three o'clock in the morning in SoHo. One cab was slowly coming toward us and I blurted out, "I'm so sorry. I was completely wrong."

She cocked her head and said, "Is this because you want that cab?" She knew it was about five hours past my bedtime and I probably would've sold my mother to get a taxi.

"No," I said, "I really am, and I don't want to fight anymore."

"Me neither," she said. "You can take the cab."

From then on, whenever a fight got too ridiculous one of us would say, "You can take the cab." It was our safe sentence and it got us through the rough years. And now that we're older and more mature, we just mostly take the bus.

CHAPTER 12
WHEN THE DOG BITES,
WHEN THE BEE STINGS

In the 1990s, I became somewhat obsessed with the movie *Total Recall,* a bit of science fiction brilliance loosely based on a Philip K. Dick story. When it came out on video, I bought it at full price and watched it over and over again. It follows Douglas Quaid, played expertly by Arnold Schwarzenegger, who, through a confluence of futuristic plot twists and turns, ends up on Mars and finds a rebel colony of people who have mutated because of poor radiation shielding on Earth. There he meets the most fascinating character in the movie, Kuato, the mutant leader of the resistance who is physically attached to his unmutated brother George. When I say "attached," I mean not like a conjoined twin, but like an ugly extra appendage. Kuato uses his clairvoyant powers to help Quaid unlock the secret to his past and the mystery of a reactor built by an ancient Martian civilization so Quaid can go save the world.

Kuato is hidden in his brother's body like a terrible secret. In the movie, when Quaid wants to talk to Kuato, George, a handsome-enough guy, slumps over, goes to sleep, and out of his abdomen pops the gooey, fetal Chucky doll–looking Kuato. He's all veiny and unfinished — not attractive. In my mind, he is George's deal breaker.

After that I started thinking of myself as having my own Kuato, but it wasn't my mutant clairvoyant rebel leader, it was all the negative feelings that I didn't want to admit I harbored. They were hidden in my sternum in the shape of an angry, slimy alien, and when I operated from my lower self, it was Kuato, not me. When I noticed a friend's dramatic weight loss and felt jealous instead of happy for them, it was Kuato. When I got a message that a friend had won an all-expense-paid trip to the Caribbean in February because she had walked into a furniture store in Long Island at the right moment and I pounded my fists and said, "WHY NOT ME?" it was all Kuato. But lest you think all that Kuato could feel was jealousy, when I found out that a friend had been turned down for a high-paying job that would have given her so much more than I had and was sad about it, Kuato celebrated her misfortune. You see, Kuato traffics in schadenfreude, too.

Essentially, Kuato was a perfect representation of all the ugly feelings that had cropped up in my friendships, despite my best efforts to contain them. He hadn't been finished, and he depended on me to feed him with my rage and bitterness. And lucky for him there was no shortage of food.

My first real job was in a talent agency. I sat with other assistants in a row of attached cubes. There were four of us: Jay, the funny gay guy; Marilyn, the woman who had gone back to work when her kids graduated; Veronique, whose sole purpose in life was to make me feel lesser; and me. The four of us were together twelve hours a day, including lunches that we ate at our desks. They became my closest friends and pretty much the only people I talked to.

And Here Was the Problem with Veronique.

Her mother was a model.

Her father was a physicist.

She looked like a model and had the brains of a physicist.

Why, oh, WHY couldn't she have the BRAINS of a model and the LOOKS of a physicist?

We were all making no money and eating Cup Noodles at our desks, except she lived with her boyfriend, The King of Wall Street. So she could afford to eat sushi out of little lacquer boxes.

Oh yeah, and she couldn't keep weight on.

One day I saw her eating and she was holding her knife and fork wrong — like an ape! I was giddy and grabbed Jay, barely containing my glee.

"Oh, that's the European way," he said coolly. "She went to school in Paris."

"Ah, that's why she speaks so many FOREIGN LANGUAGES," I retorted.

She was nice enough, but I always had the feeling when we did anything together that she would've rather been with pretty much anyone but me. There was something about us that didn't click, but you'd never know it. To the outside world we looked like pretty darn good friends.

In those days, I wore twenty-dollar Gap dresses and chunky pearl necklaces I bought from street vendors, while Veronique had hand-me-down Chanel suits. All of us were there because we wanted to become agents, or the other ones were. I didn't know what I wanted to do. We did our work, and at nine p.m., when we were finished, we'd go to some theater revue and look for talented actors we might be able to bring in and represent. Signing the right client could lead you to your big break as a theatrical agent. Veronique, though, was already friends with actors and models, and so clients would hand her people. She'd bring prospective clients in to meet the agents, and you'd hear laughter and applause coming from the office. The one time I brought someone in, I was told afterward that the person "really needed a decent haircut."

One morning I came into work and saw a young woman seated next to Veronique in her cube. I heard Veronique explaining what she did all day. ("Now, don't forget, every few hours you have to walk by Julie's desk and pull up your size double-zero pants and complain that they must size clothes on elephants these days.")

Jay walked by to get coffee and pulled me over. Apparently, a very, very famous hot young actor had left his big agency and was *signing with Veronique.* She was no longer an assistant. She was an agent. It was, in some ways, a relief to me. For the past few months I had needed to wear a belly shirt every day because I couldn't fit anything over Kuato. He just kept screaming, "WHY

DOES SHE HAVE GUCCI SUN-GLASSES AND WE HAVE SUNGLASS HUT?" It would be better for me if she was in an office with the door shut.

Later that day, the office had a party for her. Jay and I did the toast and snuck downstairs for coffee.

"I'm happy for her," he said.

"Really?" I responded. "Then we can no longer be friends."

"She worked hard."

"No she didn't! Everything was handed to her."

"Some things were, that's true, but please tell me you're not getting into the entertainment business because you believe in fairness and righteousness."

He was absolutely correct. And if I'd been her, I'd have gladly taken the same trappings. I think that my real problem with her was that she had confidence. She felt she deserved things and she got them. I felt undeserving and had no confidence. Her personality was a huge affront to me.

Not long after that, I got fired. Quite possibly my job wasn't being done perfectly because I was so busy looking at the lesser hand I'd been dealt. It was like the opposite of Jack Nicholson in *As Good As It Gets*. She made me want to be a worse person.

179

When I look back at that time, it's very clear that I was enormously insecure. It was my first job, and I was scared, but mainly I was just young. Now I am no longer in that world; I am mature and a mentally healthy human being with a clear sense of who I am. And when I see the Best Actress winner thanking Veronique at the Oscars and such, you know what? It doesn't even bother me. I can't say I'm happy for her, but give me another twenty years.

It's one thing to be envious of a friend's success, but it's more than a little disconcerting when I find myself cheering along someone's failure, like I am suddenly some barbarian screaming for a gladiator to bludgeon a wild animal in a Roman arena. Under the guise of taking her out to a nice dinner, I consulted with my close friend Claudia, a musician and psychotherapist, about the whole schadenfreude thing.

"To me, schadenfreude, and other behaviors like it, have roots in early trauma," she said, "either explicit or implicit, where a caregiver found pleasure in the discomfort or pain of the child."

"Blech!" I said eloquently.

"Early boundary violations can cause a personality disorder where the person feels a sense of meaning and control in their life only if someone they know appears to be suffering."

"Why?"

"Unconscious revenge toward the early sadist?" she said, gently spreading strawberry butter on a popover.

"Okay, now I'm totally mortified," I said. "No one was ever sadistic toward me!"

"I'm pretty sure that what you have experienced, Julie, is not Schadenfreude with a capital S," she reassured me.

"So what would you call it when I'm glad that a writer twenty years younger and ten pounds lighter than me doesn't sell as many books as I did and I'm secretly feeling gleeful?" I asked. "I mean, not that I've ever felt that, but if I did."

"That's not schadenfreude, that's being competitive, and it's not a crime," she explained. "That could have more to do with a need for survival."

Yes, I liked that explanation much better. I wasn't an animal, just a healthy friendly competitor!

There's a difference between personal and professional "competition." I think we are all more apt to forgive an ambitious worker than some conspiring bridesmaid.

When Jancee got engaged, and I'd been

181

hoping to get engaged for much longer but still had no ring, we had a big crying session. I told her I loved her and was happy for her, and she told me that her engagement wouldn't feel good until I was engaged. I couldn't convey strongly enough how happy I was for her, but we'd talked about it so much that she knew how bad I was feeling about my own somewhat stalled situation. It's something that frequently occurs, especially around engagements and pregnancies. I have had so many discussions with women who were trying to get pregnant and were crushed at the news that their sister or best friend got pregnant before they did. I had a good friend who was trying to get pregnant for years with IVF. I am sure she started way before me and she definitely disappeared when I got pregnant. When I had my baby, I asked her to meet me for lunch — not come see Violet — at Saks like we always had. She sat down at the table and with a huge smile on her face said, "How is THE BABY?" Her eyes were already filling with tears. I told her that I'd thrown the baby out because it was making too much trouble. She burst into tears and hysterical laughter at the same time. "Thank you," she said. I told her that no baby was going to bring down my dear friend. And she talked a little about her frustration, and I listened and did not feel the need to tell her how perfect Violet's toes were, and then we moved on and discussed world events, about which I knew nothing. "The Berlin Wall came down? WHEN?"

A few years later, she had beautiful twins. We took a walk around the park with them, and she told me that she would never forget that day we met for lunch just like we had before, and how I never made her feel like my having a baby was something I succeeded at and she failed at.

What I finally learned was that negative feelings are normal and natural and even healthy in a relationship, and they will always be there. But if you can find a way to get them out without acting them out, you'll be available to the good and positive feelings you have for your friends. Being emotionally mature means owning your feelings, both good and bad, and not letting them take over your life. When I see my friends accomplishing great things and I feel proud and gratified and celebratory, those are the truly transcendent moments of friendship. Ultimately, I had to let my Kuato go — not only was he negative, he was also wrecking all of my blouses.

CHAPTER 13
YOU HATE MY HUSBAND/
I HATE YOUR WIFE

When I was about eight or nine, at the age you begin to have a consciousness that the tall people in your life exist for reasons other than to give you stuff or take your stuff away, my parents' friends started splitting up. It seemed to come in like a slow tide, the news of a divorce. I'd hear my mom on her morning calls to her mother and three sisters, alternately expressing shock and admitting, "I can't believe they were together this long." Either way her attention would turn to the matter of custody. Not the couple's children, mind you, but which person in the relationship my parents would "get." According to my mother — and so, as far as I knew — every couple had a good person whom you liked and who brought wine and almond torte and laughed when they came to dinner, and a bad person who brought conversations to a screeching halt and invaded your personal space and talked

184

about their bowels. Frequently, according to my mother, my parents got stuck with the stinker. Mainly because the good one was usually the one who had done the bad thing.

Today, most of the couples I'm friends with are made up of two individuals I like, though exceptions leap to mind — LEAP! I say. If I were to show the pie chart of my brain, upward of 43 percent of it would show "Wondering why X and Y are together." This is up from .6 percent before I had a child in school. In the morning, I watch fathers dropping their kids off at school, and I come back in the afternoon and see the mothers picking them up (or vice versa). You see the two people separately, and one of them is meticulously dressed and the other is wearing stained sweats, or one of them is horsing around with the kids and the other is surgically attached to their smart phone — or one of them is a woman, and the other is clearly a gay man. And the thought starts rolling through my head, I don't see it. And that's okay. I've actually learned that couples need to have chemistry only with *each other,* not with *me.* But I digress. It really matters only when a friend's significant other is a lout.

When it comes to this subject, I consider myself an expert. In 1998, I was awarded first place in the prestigious Worst Boyfriend in All the World, Possibly Even All of History and Maybe Other Planets, Too competition. I could give you all of the details about him, but it's probably better for the sake of this discussion for you to just imagine the worst person in the world for someone you care about to date: your friend's a vegan and she's dating a hunter, or your friend is a snowman and he's dating a grill chef, or your friend is a Lorax and he's dating a Once-ler. That's how the people close to me felt about this guy. Actually, I'm worried that you haven't imagined someone bad enough. Can you go back to your person and make them just a bit worse? It wasn't just a matter of people not being able to stand "Joe" personally, they also very much wanted me to break up with him.

At the time we were, uh, courting, one of my friends was also seeing a no-goodnik. We had an understanding that we could talk to each other about our relationship woes because the other one wasn't going to say, "Get rid of him!" We empathized or chuckled knowingly. "He took all the money out of my wallet," one of us would say. "I know, same thing happened to me!" the other would reply. Unlike in our conversations with our other friends, there was no threat of lecture.

People often ask, "What were you thinking?" I can say that that woman who married one of the Menendez brothers, Safia Gaddafi, and I were all presumably thinking something along the lines of "I can't wait for my mother to meet him!" And "Sure, I know he murdered his business associate/parents/millions of innocents, but people can change!"

Both of my brothers are married to wonderful, lovely, smart, charming women, and these unions were very welcome in our family, because many of their ex-girlfriends had made my mother and the rest of us continuously smack our foreheads. Now, mind you, neither one dated any ex-convicts, but in my family not having a good sense of humor is a form of crime, so they were in fact current convicts. At least the bum I dated was funny.

When I was working at Häagen-Dazs in college, I became friends with someone I never would have known otherwise. Angelica was a former cocktail waitress and the most down-to-earth person I had ever met. There wasn't a shred of pretense to her. She had this boyfriend, a guy I'll call Al, because he looked exactly like a white Al Sharpton. She brought him to my apartment for dinner parties on a couple of occasions. He did things like feel the bread I put out to see if it was warm, and then *tsk* disappointedly when it wasn't. And then, though he was the only one who really didn't belong there, he chose to commandeer all of the table conversation, regaling us with his inimitable yarns. I think it's important here to share his top three yarns:

Yarn Number One: He worked as a custodian in a senior center where there was an elderly lady who thought his name was Ted. So day after day she'd say, "Good morning, Ted." And one day he finally said to her, "FUCK YOU, MY NAME IS AL!"

Yarn Number Two: Al had to go to the DMV and renew his Class 2 Commercial Driver's License so he could leave the door open to returning to truck driving if his hemorrhoids ever went away. So he was on line at the DMV and the woman working there, who according to Al wasn't even a native English speaker, had the nerve to ask him for his green card. Could you imagine that someone didn't recognize that he, Al, was a red-blooded, hemorrhoidal American? So he said to her, "I don't got no green card, but how 'bout I show you my DICK?"

Yarn Number Three: Jehovah's Witnesses

came to his door and asked if he wanted to hear some scripture, and he said to them, pointing, "Read my shirt." Which said: GO FUCK YOURSELF!

The thing about Al, though, was not just that he was an obnoxious racist breaker of some poor father's heart, but that he was also married and had kids. I think his wife had some awful disease, too. Somehow, Angelica didn't see him as I did, and unfortunately in that case, I had to stop being friends with her outside of the ice cream parlor.

My own roundly disliked boyfriend Joe was damaged goods. He was my first rescue dog, except he was a dog who had committed armed bank robbery. I thought that his troubled background and the fact that he'd never been in therapy or had anyone give him a break was the cause of his problems. I would introduce him to analytical thought and kindness. His father died when he was a kid, and he suffered as a result. "Lots of people suffer! They don't rob banks!" my father pointed out.

When I think back on that period, my nervous leg starts to shake. I feel a combination of anger and remorse, but I also remember the thrill of being with him.

■ ■ ■ ■

But there's doing something you know is dangerous for the thrill of it, and then there's being blithely convinced that something that is clearly problematic to everyone else is just fine. Somewhere between the age of three and four, I was playing horsie in the freshly snow-covered backyard of my best friend Rebecca's house. The game was pretty simple: I tied a winter scarf tightly around her neck and she ran around the yard as I pulled it yelling, "GO, HORSIE!" At some point her mother came screaming out the door and told us to stop and — screaming, screaming — "NEVER PUT ANYTHING AROUND ANYONE'S NECK!" I listened as we took the scarf off, but honestly I thought she'd gone completely mad. I had no idea that what we were doing was dangerous, and even after she said it, I still thought she'd gone off the deep end. It was a little blue hand-knit woolen scarf with small white snowmen scattered around it. It wasn't a knife or fire or a gun. In the years since, that moment has come back to me again and again — even in college I still thought she had over-reacted. It didn't really click until I had a kid of my own who did stupid things and scared the crap out of me. But it was the not getting it at the time and thinking that I really knew better that is poignant for me.

I'm now friends with a lot of my daughter's school friends' parents. There was one woman I really liked, and Violet liked her son. I could totally have seen us getting together socially as families, but her husband made my head explode.

He was one of those people who think they know everything and no one else does, not to mention he studied art and film and music in different grad programs, so he was a cultural snob. He would always be gifting me with his opinion, which I didn't want, or telling me about a composer or artist only he knew about, and why I couldn't possibly even conceive of the relevance and import of this person because I, like everyone who isn't him, am too stupid to be alive. One time we were hanging out with the kids at a school picnic, and I made the mistake of saying I never get to movies anymore, and he started telling me the plot of an artsy-fartsy foreign film that I had to see. I was to hire a babysitter and see this film because it was simply the most important cultural event of our time!

"Is Jennifer Aniston in it?" I asked.

" 'Cause I don't see any movies without JenAn." I added, "I just love her hair."

He sputtered at me and started talking about someone named "Mee-nu." The fact is, I was a cinema studies major at NYU. I know a thing or two about movies, but I wasn't going to get into it with him; he had so much invested in being the most knowledgeable.

I couldn't for the life of me figure out why this sweet woman put up with this pompous ass. There was no pretention about her, and that was all he was. She was in his thrall, and I wanted to throttle him. I was secretly relieved when they moved to London, because although I'd miss her and their kid, I knew those Brits would wipe the intellectual floor with him.

My aunt Mattie and I used to watch a considerable amount of daytime TV shows featuring women or men suing a former boyfriend or girlfriend for taking them for a ton of dough. Or women who repeatedly have a need for the televised revelation of the results of paternity tests. There is a woman who was on *Maury* nineteen times — NINETEEN TIMES — with nineteen different men, checking to see if any of them was the father of her kid. Think about that.

You're basically looking back on, at most, an eight-week period of time.

That means you've slept with at least nineteen men in that span of time; clearly for this woman it was more because none of them was the match. And there you are with your little eighteen-month-old baby with the elastic bow on her head, waiting to see if maybe this time you guessed right. My favorite part is the expression on the woman's face when the guy gets up and fist pumps because he's not the father. She sort of looks up and around. "Gee, I thought it was him. Hmm, so who else, who . . . else . . . ?"

Now we're talking about the minds of other people. You, gentle reader, are sane. But maybe at one point you did something that I would consider crazy. True, I dated a mobster, but I'd never jump out of a plane. Or ride in a hot air balloon. Or go on Space Mountain. Or get in a car with a person who has had too much to drink. There are lapses in judgment that can sometimes last a lot longer than we hope. And what was most important to me when I was going through it was for people to try to see what I saw, because then at least when they gave me advice, I listened. I didn't take it, but I did hear it.

What you really want to do with your friends with unfortunate partners is try to remain a good friend to them. It's a complicated and delicate situation; you don't want anyone's feelings to be hurt unnecessarily. It's also important to look at your opinion of this person and make sure you're clear about why you feel this way, and that it isn't about you. Hopefully, whatever you're seeing in this unsuitable suitor will eventually come to light for your friend, too. Those things do have a way of working out like that. And then you can be there and hold your friend's hand and tell them, "You know, I never liked him."

CHAPTER 14
THANKS, I NEEDED THAT

Whenever I hear people describe themselves as "brutally frank," I recoil. I've got to be honest, I don't really love the truth, and I definitely don't want it if it hurts me. And from a friend? It's a double "no thank you, please." I see myself as a soft cushion for my friends to land on when they return from the harshness of the world, and vice versa. If Jancee calls me and says, "I had a fight with someone," before I even hear what happened, I say, "You were right! That other person was dead wrong. They don't deserve to live in the world with you!" If it turns out that the fight was with her two-year-old, I soften it . . . a little.

I can be somewhat judgmental. It's not superficial judgment, either, like criticizing style choices. I couldn't care less if you wear black socks with sandals or whether you have gray dreadlocks down to your waist. I am not going to *tsk tsk* at your eyebrow arches or your body shape. People are all different, and how they choose to look should be only their business, as well as the business of my paternal grandmother, who took it as a personal affront if someone was what she deemed unkempt. She would come and tell us how nervy the guy stacking boxes of fruit in the supermarket was for having an untucked shirt. Anyway, she was nuts.

What I consider much more meaningful are (1) how people take care of and treat their animals, (2) how people take care of and treat their children, and (3) how people take care of and treat themselves.

The thing about watching someone else parent is that unless you suspect a child is in danger, it's very hard to challenge what someone else is doing. Perhaps because it's the most important job anyone can have, people don't really want to hear how they're doing it wrong. Most parents I see do not take the task lightly, and there are as many styles of parenting as there are runny noses in kindergarten. Before I had Violet, I was very clear on who was a good parent and who was not. I could not believe the way certain people disciplined their kids or didn't, or that people I knew were so inconsistent. I thought I knew the truth, but really it was just my opinion. There is no one more self-righteous about child rearing than a person without kids, except possibly grand-parents.

When Jancee had her sweet little baby girl, Sylvie, Violet was six. So whatever I think I had sort of known about parenting a new-born, I'd forgotten by then. When Violet was born I was quite obsessed with what was going to happen with the belly button. Books said the belly button fell off, and for some reason the thought of that was disturb-ing to me. I'd never heard that before, and I worried that other things would fall off, too. When I asked my sister-in-law, who had two daughters, what happened to it, she said, "Hmm, I don't know." Then she asked her mother, who had been a neonatal nurse, and she also couldn't quite remember. The funny thing is right now I'm trying to remember and I can't. It's not in the charts of milestones and therefore doesn't have a lot of weight in people's memories.

Anyway, I Googled the belly button thing before I went to visit Jancee because I was sure the question would be plaguing her, too. It wasn't. The only thing I really had to share with her was confidence. When some-one has their first baby, they hold it like it's a glass ornament and then someone with bigger kids comes in and starts tossing it around like a Hacky Sack. Jancee was so open and questioning, and willing to listen to my opinions. I told her that for the first few days everyone else seems like they are experts, but in a short time you become the expert. You know what your baby's cries mean, and you give the comfort. I knew I could advise her, and I knew her well enough to know that she'd always be open to it. I speculated that everyone would be telling her what to do and how to do it, and that they will all say that she should appreciate this time with her baby because it goes too fast. They mean well, but as anyone with a sleepless newborn can tell you, that time ain't goin' fast.

For some reason, my generation of parents has been all about the sleep training. My mother said, "When I had a baby we put them in their room, they went to sleep, and that was it." She will say incredulously, "Now they've got an entire section of Barnes and Noble devoted to how to get a kid to sleep." If you have a newish baby that doesn't sleep, you see anyone with a sleeping baby as the keeper of the Holy Grail. Violet was a preemie, so she ate slowly and by the time she finished eating she was about ready to start again. I was completely out of my mind for lack of sleep, and it didn't work to just sleep when she did, because I couldn't fall asleep in five seconds like she could. It was excruciating. I fantasized about situations where I'd be able to sleep, like maybe in jail. And I was so tired and cuckoo that I couldn't read the books that allegedly had the answers. But I'd read little parts of them, the parts that pertained to me. I'd read them over and over, and they would say: "If you do this, your baby will sleep." But my baby couldn't read, so she didn't know that. I was becoming a basket case.

I had a new friend at the time, Susan, who had a baby who was five months younger than mine and colicky. If I was going crazy, Susan was, well, also going crazy. But she had success in letting her little girl cry it out until she slept. And so during that time, she was the expert. She told me what I had to do, but I couldn't stand it. If Violet cried and I didn't go to her, I reasoned that she'd think I didn't love her and she'd have to go to baby therapy. During the day, I'd read about how babies who couldn't go to sleep themselves would develop into insomniacs. They'd be unproductive in their lives, a bunch of Marlon Brandos from *On the Waterfront*. I was all for the notion of co-sleeping, but she didn't sleep when she was in my bed, she lay there with her big saucer eyes wide open and looking at this incompetent person who was supposed to be her mother. Day after day I'd complain to Susan, and finally she really yelled at me to let Violet cry it out. She did say something like, "Either you have to do it or you have to stop complaining about it." She was very strong and she promised me that I could call her while the crying was going on.

That night I tried, but I was sure that she was crying because she had a button stuck in her throat and was going to suffocate, so I burst in and ended up doing the whole stupid up-all-night thing again. The next day, Susan wrote down on an index card: DO NOT GO IN. SHE IS NOT CHOKING. That night I sat outside the room. I wouldn't call Susan. If Violet was crying like that, I would do nothing to numb my own pain; I wanted her cries to hurt me as much as they hurt her. I think she went on for several hours, but eventually she went to sleep. And lo, the heavens opened up and she started being a baby who slept at night. I really admired Susan for making me take that advice. It wasn't as if I thought I knew anything, as a new parent; the only thing you're really sure you know is nothing. But you know what feels right, and listening to your baby cry does not feel right.

The other magical advice I didn't take and then finally did was swaddling my newborn. The first night home I didn't swaddle her, and she was awake the entire night. I think I didn't swaddle her because . . . I was afraid she'd have to scratch her nose and she wouldn't be able to. That was true, too, she wouldn't be able to, because BABIES CAN'T SCRATCH THEIR NOSES BECAUSE THEY CAN'T DO ANYTHING. I also knew because of sudden infant death syndrome that you weren't supposed to put a blanket in the bassinet with a baby, so how could you swaddle it in a blanket? I gave birth so early I got to go to only one Lamaze class, and was sure I had missed all the significant information. I think they had one whole class called "Don't Kill Your Baby." Then my friend John came over, a neonatal physical therapist. He swaddled her like a tight, little rugelach, and boom, she went to sleep. I said, "Uh, what about blanket death?" And he said, "I'm more concerned about mother death if you don't get some sleep."

There's a fine line, or maybe it's a fat four-lane highway, between offering helpful advice and harping on something until your friend wants to choke you. In fact, I think you want to be very careful about picking any friend who considers themselves an expert in anything you like to do regularly — like eat, or wear clothes.

Several years ago I made friends with a lovely, caring woman, Gussy. She is, how should we say, *obsessed* with what goes into her body. When I first met her, she didn't eat anything "white" (sugar, flour, milk, cocaine), and every time I saw her she tried to push her tattered copy of *Sugar Blues* on me.

"Read this it will change your life," she'd say in one long string.

Is there anything that makes you not want to read something more than hearing it will change your life? I have a long list of life-changing books that I will never, ever read.

"You could have at least bought me a new copy," I said. "I don't want your old bathtub-stained book."

"If I get you a new one, will you read it?"

"No."

"That's why I didn't buy one — because I knew you wouldn't."

"So then why don't you stop asking me?"

She put the book back in her purse, waiting for the next time she'd take no for an answer.

Whenever she walks into my kitchen, she picks up every box, can, or package and scans the ingredients, shaking her head and slapping her forehead, *tsk*ing, muttering in Yiddish. Sometimes if I know she's coming over I'll stop at the deli and get a box of pink Hostess Sno Balls just to give her a little something to do.

About two years ago she became a vegetarian, but she couldn't just be a vegetarian, she had to try to make me a vegetarian. Then she went vegan or, as we say, "vegan except for the things that she likes to eat that aren't vegan."

We have another friend who has said she never coughs in Gussy's presence because then she'll have to hear an hour lecture about the evils of dairy and its diabolical contribution to the creation of phlegm.

I have my own food issues, so I really don't need anyone else's. I've told her to stop it in the most loving of ways, and now when she starts I just gently put my hands around her throat and she says, "Okay, okay." And she stops, but not without muttering, "It's your life. . . ." I do love her. I hope I don't have to kill her.

I have another friend, Debbi, who does this same relentless noodging with clothes. She works in the fashion industry and the first thing she does when she sees me is size me up. It's like I'm on one unending episode of *What Not to Wear.*

In my daily life, it's true, I do wear mostly jeans and T-shirts and sneakers. I also have a habit of falling in love with one T-shirt and wearing it until the people around me have to stage an intervention. My feet are terrible — not just bad foot problems but they are hideous. Like I'm afraid for children to see them, and, oh yeah, *I work from home and have a kid and dogs, none of which require an Armani suit and kitten heels!*

Despite knowing all these things about me, if Debbi comes in and sees me in my "uniform," she'll give me hints on fashionable casual clothes. When I'm cold at home I put on a Peanuts sweatshirt that I got for my twenty-sixth birthday, approximately many years ago. Debbi suggests that I wear my jeans and T-shirt if I have to, but how about a baby blue cashmere wrap instead? She also sends me JPEGs of Gwyneth Paltrow in her daywear, which looks very similar to mine except expensive and glamorous, and by the way, she's got a staff of stylists, and she's frequently photographed, and also by the way, I'm not Gwyneth Paltrow. It's not that I don't appreciate Debbi's advice . . . except that I don't.

These well-intentioned noodges make me think twice about counseling anyone who isn't in immediate danger of having an anvil fall on their head. The only really necessary advice is "GET OUT OF THE WAY!"

When it comes to how people care for their animals, however, I'm not quite so polite. If I see something wrong, I do say something. I'm not talking about the woman who has her Jack Russell in a leather jacket and motorcycle cap. I mean, that's wrong, but I realize there's a world of people who think it's not. So I let them have their silly dog clothes. But I call them on what I see as seriously bad behavior.

When I see friends treating their pets questionably, it's touchier. When one friend told me she was declawing her cat and wanted me to say it was okay, I told her I couldn't. I just don't think amputating an animal's toes is okay. I also am very anti–ear cropping and anti–tail docking. It makes me crazy, and people who know me already know it. No one asks my opinion on those issues. And anyone who knows me doesn't ask me for pet training advice, either, because my dogs are kind of badly behaved. But I do get asked for advice on more of the emotional issues related to dogs, and I have to tread lightly.

When I was working as a reporter a number of years ago, I was at a big celebrity party. I interviewed a famous starlet and we started talking dogs. It turned out she lived near me with her pug, Alvy. I told her about my Boston terrier, Otto, and before I knew it we had a date to walk our dogs together.

The next day we met on the corner of a busy street near the park. She came walking up with her Starbucks cup and Alvy. I was trying to figure out what kind of leash she had that was so thin I couldn't see it, when I realized she didn't have one.

"Where's his leash?" I asked innocently.

"Oh, he's great!" she remarked confidently. "He doesn't need a leash. He always stays with me."

I didn't know what to say. People who walk their dogs in the city without leashes are like the top rung of my personal WANTED list. But I just closed my mouth and kept quiet.

As we walked to the park, I saw Alvy narrowly miss being hit by a car and walk up to a giant rottweiler who snarled and growled at him. Both times the actress called him and snapped her fingers, which did nothing. Finally we got to the park and my heart relaxed a little.

Alvy plopped on her lap. I could see why

she thought he wasn't going to go anywhere off the leash, but what I explained to her then is that they're animals. I told her stories of dogs being spooked and getting hit by cars because they weren't on leashes, and she just nodded knowingly and said, "That wouldn't happen with Alvy."

I wanted to be her friend more than I'd like to say, and so we kept meeting for about a week. I couldn't figure out how she didn't see how often Alvy was in danger. But to be honest, she was a little self-obsessed. I think she also thought forgoing the leash was kind of bohemian and earthy.

The next week I told her I couldn't walk with her unless she put Alvy on a leash. I said I was sorry but it made me too nervous. She sputtered some profanity and swiftly hung up on me. Her career kind of went downhill after that. I don't think it was a coincidence.

Advising someone about safety issues is pretty cut and dried, but other matters aren't. Certainly the hardest part of having a dog is that you may find yourself in the position of having to make life choices for them. God, my heart aches for anyone who is going through that. There's no right answer; it's a very painful and personal decision, but one that people frequently want help with. In those times, I try very hard to guide a friend toward finding their own answer.

When my friend called me from Washington to talk about her senior dog, Webster, I knew the turmoil she was in. We spoke for a long time, and she told me the problems he'd been having. My eyes burned as I realized she was heading toward putting him down. I tried to be as comforting as I could, recalling the things I'd found helpful when faced with my own dogs' endings. But as I listened further, I realized she wasn't in fact ready, and Webster wasn't in pain, which is the one factor that's hard to dismiss. I switched tacks and told her that the right time would reveal itself to her, and that she shouldn't feel pressured by anyone. She was so happy; I had no idea that's what she'd been needing. Usually when people call me it's because they're feeling horribly guilty about making a decision to end their pup's life, but this was different. It would be a little over a year before Webster was in the kind of shape where it really was no longer a question. But she put him down and felt secure about having done it at the right time.

I was recently having coffee with a friend

of mine, Laurie, who's a schoolteacher. The mother of one of her former students had come to her with a problem. Her child felt like her new teacher hated her, and the data made it seem that she might be right. Laurie had purposely placed this child with this teacher, who was a friend of hers, younger and less experienced but very good for the type of academics the child struggled with. Laurie felt more than a little responsible. The kid was very sweet and sensitive, and the teacher had what she described as a sarcastic streak.

She told me, "Little kids don't understand sarcasm."

I was so amazingly impressed because Laurie took it upon herself to tell this teacher what she thought. She took her out for lunch and told her she thought she was great, but she'd observed this thing happening and it was not so great. She said to her, "You gotta cut this out."

I had a knot in my stomach when she was telling me, flashing back to when I was fourteen and babysitting and a mother told me that I was too bossy with her kid. It was mortifying.

"What did she say?" I asked.

"She thanked me," Laurie said. "She had no idea she was doing it."

A lot of times people don't realize how they're coming across, and sometimes you need to tell them. In the case of this woman, it was about her job. I think coming from Laurie made a big difference, too. Laurie is a mature, well-respected teacher, but the younger woman could easily have felt judged and told her to take a hike. I gave her a lot of credit for taking in the advice, and from what I heard, she changed, too.

There's no better outcome than that, and we need friends who tell it to us straight, even when we might not want to hear it. Sometimes it happens, sometimes you get clobbered, because sometimes the truth really does hurt.

CHAPTER 15
ABSENCE MAKES THE HEART WORK HARDER

I know about the pain and heartache of long-distance friendships. When I was four, I was ripped out by the roots of the home where I'd lived since I was born. From the window in my room, I could see into my best friend Rebecca's room. When we moved thirty-one minutes north, to a giant house in the middle of nowhere, I couldn't see my best friend Rebecca's room from my window anymore.

For the next several years we tried achingly to remain BFFs, but when your age is in the single digits, you can't really control your destiny so well. In other words, it was a pain in the ass for our moms to drive us to each other's houses, and over time the expanse of the Saw Mill River Parkway defeated us.

I'd like to think that now that I'm an adult and can drive and buy my own Amtrak tickets, I have mastered the art of minimizing distances and no friendship suffers from our not being in the same time zone, but it's just not true. I blame it on that first experience with Rebecca; I tend to believe no matter how hard you try, staying in touch when there is distance is tough. Also, I'm so goddamn lazy.

When I'm feeling down, my friend Patty cheers me up by saying, "Do you want to make a dinner plan with me and cancel it?" I'll admit, it brings me momentary glee. In order to get everything done and retain some semblance of sanity, I can go out only so many times a day. Four dog walks and two school trips and I'm already at six. Something else is bound to happen (a dearth of milk) and I'm up to seven. That's when my image starts to blur like Zelig. Come evening, when most people with jobs can finally do something, I'm in comfies sans bra. When I have plans, I get weepy. "I have to get dressed again?" "Do I have to put on mascara?" Sometimes, on a particularly magical night, I'll think I have to go to something and it will be canceled and I'll act like I got a stay from the governor.

The sad reality is that there is one aspect of friendship I just totally suck at, and that's getting together with people. And if you have friends, you know that every so often they want to see your pretty face in person.

People admire in others what isn't easy for themselves. I marvel at those who are good at long-distance friendships. I have a friend who hates to exercise; once a year she becomes obsessed with marathoners. "It's like running for the bus for the entire day!" Well, only the entire day if you're not a great marathoner . . .

When a friend moves from Manhattan to Brooklyn, in my world the friend might as well have moved to Mozambique. I may not be perfect at close-distance friendship, but I am completely dreadful at long distance.

I always thought of it as sort of a given that we all accepted. "Julie doesn't like to go out at night. Julie doesn't really travel." Like you'd talk about an agoraphobe or someone allergic to shellfish. I blame it on my aunt Mattie. When all of our family members started moving to Vermont, Washington, D.C., Maine, New Hampshire, and Boston, she said to me, "We're from New York. We all came from here and they left. They should have to visit us." We stayed here! We kept our end of the bargain! With family, you can say, "I'm not traveling to you, you have to come to me." But you can't really get away with that with friends.

After graduating from NYU, my friend

Barbara's sister Kristin moved to Brooklyn. I figured I'd never see her again. I think she had been living there for about six months when Barbara said, "You really need to come see Kristin's apartment." I tried my "Why should I, she's the one who moved" spiel, but it fell on deaf ears.

"We'll go together," she decided. "You might actually like it."

It turned out that Kristin's Brooklyn apartment, though nearly fifty minutes from my place, was very nice. Her neighborhood was pleasant and friendly, like a little village with a lot of pottery and muffin stores. I patted myself on the back big-time for traveling all that way, and got only slightly annoyed when it was time to leave and we had to take the subway home late because a car service would have been really expensive.

Not long after that, I had a friend move to Connecticut. I thought I was going to have a breakdown. Connecticut is a whole other state, with different laws and everything! I had just read an article about Connecticut in my podiatrist's office (exotic, wild Connecticut). There is a law there that a pickle cannot be called a pickle unless it can bounce. What if I brought a limp pickle into Connecticut? Would I go to Pickle Jail? I bravely took the train up, though, and dutifully smiled through my fear. I even brought banana bread (there were no banana bread laws, as far as I knew). And it really wasn't all that much of a sacrifice; she lived in a beautiful house with a pool and barbecued for me. I even made plans to come back again!

Those were my only two big long-distance friendships until I was in my thirties and there was a mass exodus from New York City among my friends. For many people, New York City is a place to live before your real life begins, and then you move to somewhere with a house and a car. But for me, the city would always be home. And thus began a new phase of life, one in which I was forced to maintain long-distance friendships or risk losing them.

As friends moved to Seattle, Los Angeles, Portland, Chicago, New Hampshire, Orlando, and the UK, I found myself working harder and harder to stay in contact, especially before Facebook and texting. I railed against the cruel world that had made different time zones so I couldn't wake up at seven and call a friend and have it be the same time where they are. I actually ripped a page out of the phone book that had a map overlaid with time zones, but I didn't make a lot of money and those long-distance calls were still expensive. Plus it was hard to get people on the phone. I wrote a lot of letters, and I had a very healthy correspondence going with many friends. A box of those letters remains in my closet today. I also made cassette tapes in case any of my friends missed my self-involved ramblings. I kept in touch pretty religiously, and so did my friends . . . initially. And then the time between letters got longer and longer. Maintenance really is the hard part. There is a big difference between friends who are local and friends who are not. There's a definite hole that is filled by friends who are in the area. They can come to your party or meet you for lunch or go with you to a horrible doctor's appointment or come look at the yellow dress you're considering for that thing you have to go to that you wish was canceled. The long-distance friends are different. They can talk about stuff, but they're just not there for the nitty-gritty, and the lapses of time make talking about the minor stuff of everyday life hard.

I know we all have friends who make us feel like a year could go by and we'd still start talking as if we'd just seen each other yesterday. And if you're in a period of life when there aren't a lot of changes, that might be true. But if you've had a lot going on, it can be hard to box it up into a neat story. When I was trying to get Violet into a good public school, there was a dramatic update almost daily, but later when I told the story to friends living out of town it came out something like, "Violet was in a bad school and we wanted to switch her to a different school and then we did." Not exactly a cliffhanger.

I have a few close long-distance friends, including Vesna, my former film school pal who is somehow now a doctor; Mae, whom I interned with years ago; and Kristin, who after that momentous move to Brooklyn left again and moved to someplace called "New Hampshire."

Mae, who was originally from San Diego, lived with me briefly when we were interning together, and of all the people I know in the world, she is the one most likely to make me laugh until I pee. She moved out West after living in New York. We are both bad at keeping in touch and she got married right after she moved, and then started her family, and I, well . . . I was just very busy with deciding whether to order Mexican or Thai food for dinner. It could be years before one of us gets inspired to pick up the phone, and whenever we do, we don't talk much about what's going on in our lives. I usually ask her how many kids she's up to (it's something like forty) and then we start reminiscing about the things that cracked us up twenty-five years ago, and we're on the floor laughing again and saying we need to see each other or keep in better contact. And we don't. I think there's a value in having someone who in your mind is stalled in a time of your life, before things got complicated. I like that when we talk we essentially think of each other as twenty-one-year-olds whose only problem is whether people can see how much cover-up we spackled over a zit.

Vesna lived in New York City all during college. She was from Chicago, and after school she moved to Los Angeles but has since settled in Portland (the one in Oregon with a wildly different time zone, not the relatively convenient one in Maine). She has always been good about calling. I adore her, and I'm so happy she excels at keeping in touch, because as I may have mentioned, it is not my strong suit. When I call her, it's usually because something medical has reminded me of her. A couple of months ago, the day before I was leaving for a two-week trip, I was stretching after a run. I felt a bump behind my knee. Of course I assumed it was a malignant tumor, and that I was being punished for traveling. I went home and called my runner friends, and everyone knew it was a Baker's cyst. I immediately checked in with Dr. Google and it was possible the cyst was nothing and would go away, or it would burst into my bloodstream and kill me. I called Vesna and told her I was dying again, and she explained that if she was my doctor she would do nothing. I told her I was going on a trip and I was kind of looking forward to it, so it was possible I was being punished.

"You know, Julie, what so few people understand about medicine," she said, "is that disease visits itself on people because they've either behaved badly or thought too highly of themselves."

"Or looked forward to a trip?"

"Yes," she said, "that's a big one."

See why I love her? Vesna's had a huge career change from film producer to doctor, gotten married, divorced, and become a single parent, enormous life-altering milestones, and I'm grateful that she's kept me in the loop for all of them. After her divorce, she traveled the world and sent frequent e-mails detailing where she was and what she was feeling. It helped me feel like I wasn't missing something. She occasionally admonishes me for not reciprocating. "Okay, how come you didn't tell me you had another book out? I had to find out by walking through Powell's?"

"I posted it on Facebook!" I say defensively.

When I spoke to her about why our long-distance friendship has worked so well — because it obviously wasn't due to me — she said, "Well, I have never found any difference in a friend that lives next door versus the friend that lives far away. Since there is no importance placed on the distance for me, I treat every friendship equally." She is smart like Albert Einstein; there is no time and space.

She also admits that the fact that she likes talking on the phone — and is good at it — doesn't hurt. "I prefer face-to-face but can still feel comfortable fully disclosing my feelings on the phone." That's true; she told me the whole story of her marriage and its dissolution over a very long phone conversation. "It's not my first choice, but sometimes it's all I've got."

She said she also sees the friends in her life as vital and assumes she is that important to them — having a strong sense of yourself is key to being good at keeping up with faraway friends. I've often wondered if someone I'm thinking of calling will want to talk to me or even remember me. Or, if they haven't kept in touch, it's because they don't really like me anymore (or never did).

The Internet was really invented to keep long-distance friendships intact. When I joined Facebook and found Kathi and Kathy, two friends from freshman year of college, it was like something magic to me. Before that, I used to look at Internet white pages, but if you didn't know what state a person was in, you couldn't really find them. Also, you may want to be in touch with someone or see what they're up to but not feel close enough to call them.

Kristin, though, is not a Facebook user, and she's not a big e-mailer (she's one of those people who doesn't check their e-mail every day, in contrast to me, who checks my e-mail constantly and even looks at it in the middle of the night if I get up to pee). Keeping up that friendship is more of a challenge because I can't rely on my technology crutch. Kristin does visit New York, and I have visited her in New Hampshire, but mostly we are kept up to date through information from her sister, and my friend, Barbara. Often when I tell Barbara something, she tells me she'll let Kristin know for me. It's like a service she provides. Like a publicist or something.

I polled a large group of people about their challenges in friendship and the majority said a significant one was maintenance with long distance. It's one thing to have the energy to do a holiday card, it's another to have more regular consistency. We're lazy by nature (when I say "we," of course I mean "I"), and mostly it's easiest to deal with what's in front of our faces. And I'd never want keeping up with friends to be an item on a to-do list. They deserve more.

A number of years ago I had a friend who lived in New York and married a French guy. Neither of them wanted to move to the other's country (this might have been a sign that they weren't really on board for this whole marriage thing) so they did the long-distance romance, and I remember how dreamy and thrilling it was when she traveled to him in Paris or he came to her in New York, showing up with giant bouquets of fragrant gardenias and wine and *chocolat.* I used to watch her and try to figure out how I could adapt that enthusiasm with my long-distance platonic friendships. Obviously in a romantic relationship there is a different element keeping you together.

But a friendship has to start with a mutual

commitment to keeping things going. If all of the responsibility rests on one person, it's not going to make it. And no matter how lousy you are at it, you've got to work in "real life" visits. A phone call or e-mail can never be as long as a dinner or several events over a few days. Ideally, you share the burden of travel. In this case, I can't use myself as an example because, to date, I suck at it. But I do recognize people who excel in traveling for friends. Barbara, for one, is quite brilliant at it. Once a year, she actually visited a friend who'd moved to Germany (Germany! That's so much farther than Brooklyn!), and the friend came here once a year to visit her. It doesn't sound like a lot of time, but adding the days up, fourteen is more than I see many of my local friends in a year. She takes long-distance friendships very seriously. "I wouldn't want someone to feel like I'd forgotten them," she told me. "I certainly would hate to feel forgotten by someone." Which is why she uses her limited number of vacation days and hard-earned frequent-flyer miles to visit people. It's not cheap and it's not easy, but it's such a moving gesture and, pun intended, it goes a long way.

A few days ago, I found myself on a school bus to Queens with my daughter's class. We were headed for the New York Hall of Science, which if you haven't been fourteen times, is really fabulous. If you do go, I highly recommend traveling there on a bus filled with third-graders who will shout over your head, "What's the grossest thing you ever barfed up?"

I had no business going to this — I had a ton of work to do and had already lost a week when Violet had her tonsils and adenoids out and did not, as I imagined she would, lay prostrate in bed for a week, quietly recovering. At the very last minute, though, another parent had to cancel and the trip was dependent on chaperones, and Violet looked up at me when the teachers asked if I could go, and I said, "Sure."

Instead of hearing the finer points of interesting vomit, I was happy to get a text from Barbara. She asked me if we could get together, she had some news to tell me. I immediately panicked.

ME: R U OK??
BARBARA: Yes! I'm fine!
ME: Is it bad news or good news?
BARBARA: Kind of both.
ME: I can see you this wknd but I don't think I cn wait to hear.
BARBARA: I can call you.

ME: I'm on a class trip on bus.
BARBARA: I can call you tonight.
ME: Are you moving?
BARBARA: Yes.
ME: ☹

Barbara and I had lived together in Manhattan since college; we had been best friends since fifth grade. We had always lived close to each other.

BARBARA: Don't you want to hear the good news?
ME: Yeah.
BARBARA: I'm going to start my own design firm! I'll have lots of clients in New York, so I'll be here a lot.
ME: Are you moving to NH? [Kristin and their parents all lived there.]
BARBARA: I need to. Kristin is going to help me with this.
ME: Oh well, I'm very happy for you but sad for me. [I'm repeating the text of this conversation so you can see how elegantly I handled this news and maybe learn something. Like what not to do.]
BARBARA: Don't be sad, it'll be great!
ME: Great for you.
BARBARA: How about if every time I come to visit I bring you a present?

ME: I'm not Violet! [Though I know my re-action was making it a little hard to tell.]

BARBARA: Julie! Didn't you just interview me about how good I am at long-distance friendships?

ME: Yeah but I didn't mean you should try it out on me!

BARBARA: Sigh.

ME: Listen, I appreciate your need to move but this isn't a good time for me. I'll reconsider your request in a year. Thank you for inquiring.

BARBARA: ☹

ME: It's fine really. I've just made a new friend on this bus. Auggie can drool almost to his knee and then snap it up.

BARBARA: There you go, see? Making lem-onade already!

ME: AUGGGHHHHHH!

Later, as I walked through The Mysteries of the Eyeball and The Journey of the Atom and The Mirrors of Craziness, Barbara texted me little hopeful messages: "I bet we'll see each other more than we do now." "I won't be so busy, so it won't take me six hours to respond to your e-mail, we can have conversations!"

I stopped being bratty and told her I was very happy for her and proud of what she

226

was doing, but inside I felt like crying. I had been struggling with some stuff in my life and just wasn't feeling like hearing that my best friend was leaving town. But I kept it to myself and plopped myself in a model race car and wrote to tell her how much I loved her, and promised that though I hadn't been very good at long-distance friendships, I felt sure that with her teaching me I'd be better.

Violet and her friends gathered around me to request a move to the next exhibit. I mentioned to Violet that Barbara told me she was moving,

"WAHH!" she fake cried.

"That's just what I said." I smiled.

"Who's Barbara?" her friend Joey asked.

"Barbara is my mom's BFF. They've been friends since they were in fifth grade."

"Yup," I said, "and we will be friends forever and ever."

"WOW!" the kids replied.

A few nights later, I went to dinner with Barbara. When we sat down, I ordered a white wine spritzer and told the waiter to keep 'em coming. Barbara gently started explaining why she was moving. She wanted to run her own business, and she wanted time to do her music (she's an amazing guitar player and singer). I agreed that it made sense, and I told her I'd be supportive in every way I could. She pulled something out of her bag and slid it across the table to me. It was a calendar she'd printed up from when she was moving through the next twelve months. Every three weeks from Friday to Sunday she wrote: *Visit Julie.* I gulped back some tears, took out my pen and crossed out one of them and wrote: *Julie visits Barbara.* We both knew, thanks to her, that this was going to be okay.

CHAPTER 16
YOU'VE GOT TO HAVE FRIENDS

A few weeks ago I was leaving my aunt Mattie's apartment with Violet on a Saturday night. My brother and his family had come into town and were staying there for a couple of days. I was really tired. It had been one of the longest weeks of my life; Paul had been working at a new job and was at the office seven days a week late into the evenings, and he wasn't getting home until after Violet and I were in bed.

I was spending a lot of time with Violet and the dogs and not enough with my work and my own thoughts — and no time at all with my friends. Violet and Paul were originally going to spend Saturday together so that I would get to take a break and meet Laura and Ann for dinner, but things had changed and he had to meet with a director. I called my stable of two babysitters, but neither was available and then I just gave in and made plans to go to my aunt's.

I was happy to see my family. I love them, and Violet thinks her cousins are the rock stars of the universe. By the time we were leaving, I just wanted to get home and get into bed. We crossed Third Avenue but there were no cabs, and as I watched the uncharitable traffic, I could feel my will weakening.

"Let's go in front of Bloomingdale's," I said to Violet, holding her hand. "Someone is bound to be getting out of a cab there."

We stood in front of Bloomingdale's until I realized it was closed and people wouldn't be taking cabs there. Violet started telling me some long story about a game she and my nieces had invented, when I saw a cab pulling up and turning on its "available" light.

"Here's one!" I grabbed the door handle while a woman got out. A guy was waiting for her on the curb, and I was afraid he was going to fight me for the cab (he would have lost). But luckily for him, he was just meeting this woman.

"Oh my God!" he said, tears in his eyes. "Whitney!"

"I know, honey!" she said, embracing him as I pulled the cab door shut. The little taxi TV popped on and as I gave our address and Violet looked for the button to turn it off, I saw the news flash: Whitney Houston had died. While Violet chatted, I pulled out my cell phone and pressed 4, Jancee's speed dial. Her voice mail picked up. In one word, I blurted, "Ohmygodjancewhitneyhouston-died!"

We got home and Paul was there. I grabbed the dogs to take them out and my cell phone rang. It was Jancee.

I picked up the phone and said, "I know, I know."

As I walked the dogs through the darkling park, the whole world full of the stresses of the past week vanished and it was just Jancee and me and a moment in pop culture that reminded us of how long we had been friends and how many things we had shared.

"Jul, remember when I interviewed her the last time?"

"Yeah, you said her voice was going then."

"It was," she recalled. "She was losing the power."

"Remember that show we were at — was it something for VH1, where she was wearing that green unitard thing?"

Jancee chuckled. "Oh yeah, she was so skinny she looked like a grasshopper."

"Yeah," I said, "but, man, remember that voice."

"She was so gorgeous, too."

Every so often we said, "I cannot believe

it." And Jancee reminded me that I'd called her when Michael Jackson died. She was in New Jersey at her parents' house and her father had come bursting into the room and said, "Farrah Fawcett died." A little while later I called her, and she said to her dad with me on the phone, "Dad, you didn't tell me about Michael Jackson! Do you know what it means to bury the lede?"

"Oh yeah," he murmured, "he died, too."

"I always feel better hearing about these things from you," she said.

We started listing the celebrities who had died since we'd been friends and the way we shared the moments when we found out with the exact same level of feeling. We didn't like to get too dramatic; these were not our families. They were significant, but we weren't going to lay flowers at the steps of their record company. But in some ways these were the people who had shaped parts of our lives, whose music had helped define our youth. We wanted to talk about them and what they meant to us and not involve the whole world. We wanted to talk about it only with each other.

Back when Jancee worked at *Rolling Stone* and we had our endless phone calls, celebrities would walk through her office regularly. She interviewed absolutely everyone, so I always felt like I had a special line on people. She knew stuff about them. We knew.

I had plopped down on a bench, and an hour went by and we finally wrapped up our call and promised to figure out a date for lunch in the next couple of weeks, and just before she hung up I said, "Jance."

"Yeah, Jul."

"I believe the children are our future."

She laughed and said good-bye. I walked back into my building feeling like I'd been completely revitalized.

The next day I called her. She answered the phone and said, "Don't tell me, Taylor Dayne?"

"I have to call you sometimes when no celebrity dies or you're going to dread me."

We had a long talk about how much we needed to talk to each other and get to be ourselves and not the rigidly defined roles of mom and wife and professional. When we talked on the phone we were single, for a little while. We were individuals.

If you ever want a quote about friendship, you're in good shape, because there are a bazillion trillion jillion of them. Sixty percent are from Winnie-the-Pooh. The other forty percent are written by Anonymous, who spent so much time writing bon mots about friends he could not possibly have had time to have any.

To summarize: Friends are good. You need them. You have to be a friend to have a friend. Agreed, but it's all sort of like saying, "If you want to be a grown-up, just get married, get a job, and have kids." It is more complicated than that. There are times when you feel so spent on your spouse or your mother or your kids or your job that you think you just want to crawl under a rock. But as soon as you connect with a friend instead, you find yourself tickled to be a part of this relationship that is so key to your emotional well-being. One of the truly amazing things about a friendship is it's something you and this person have created for yourselves together. You have to build it. You don't get friends automatically like you do family members, and there is a good deal of work in these relationships of choice. I remember watching the patron saint of relationships, Donald Trump, talking about why he divorced . . . someone, and he said it was too much work, and if a relationship is that much work, he doesn't want it. Is it any wonder he's such a hit with the ladies? We're all just looking for a man who enters a relationship fully committed to not having to do anything. I don't think most people think like Donald Trump, but I do think that people tend to put work into the category of things that are required before the things that are optional. Like school. Like jobs. Like family. It took me a long time to realize that in the list of priorities, I put the care of friendships pretty far down. It wasn't conscious, it was just always the thing I would let go. Why? Because it wasn't demanding anything from me. If I canceled on a friend, I wouldn't lose a paycheck, and they wouldn't torture me with guilt. So the people I cared so much about got the least amount of effort I could muster. I was on a long run one day when I saw the name of a friend come up on my cell phone and I clicked "dismiss" instead of "answer." It suddenly hit me that while I needed and loved my friends, I had been taking them for granted. I started thinking about all the times in my life when I was depressed or lonely, when I didn't know what to do about relationships — when I needed my friends. I thought about the future, when my parents got older, and whom I would rely on for support.

I was hitting "dismiss" on my friendships too often, and really they were the most valuable assets in my life.

But what I realized that night I called Jancee was that what had prompted my call wasn't a moment when I thought, Gee, I should really get in touch with Jancee; I wonder what Sylvie is up to. Though I do wonder that, too. But this wasn't even a thought; it was almost an involuntary response, like a breath. I remembered that feeling from high school, running into my kitchen and not even putting down my book bag, just grabbing the phone and stretching the cord too far and dialing Barbara's number. Because we had to talk about that really funny thing that happened on the bus, and it couldn't wait. And then we'd move on to more important things at hand, like what we wanted to happen that day on *General Hospital.*

"What do we need to do? Do we need to have a set monthly date?" Jancee said. "It's too long between visits. Maybe we just need to have something on the calendar."

I agreed. I didn't want to let months go by. Though the fortunate thing was now that we were in our mid-forties, celebrity deaths were coming a lot more quickly.

"Jul."

Yes, Jance.

"You don't have to wait for a celebrity to die to call," she said.

236

"I know."

"Like you can call when they go into rehab."

"You're right," I said. "I totally missed an opportunity with Demi Moore and the whip-its."

We then discussed the actresses who were our age and getting too much plastic surgery, surmising the fact that Demi Moore looked better than everyone else might be a case for doing whip-its. (I know, very twisted, but that's why we're friends.)

And it's why *your* best friends are *your* best friends. There's a certain confluence of magical elements in the chemistry that turns a person into *your* person, *your* friend.

During the past year of writing this book, I talked to my friends about our friendships, I listened to strangers tell about what works and doesn't work in their friendships, but most significantly, I lived what I was writing about in my own friendships every day.

The past year was a little rocky for me personally. There were days when I woke up and thought, I just don't know how it's all going to work out. On more than one occasion, I thought, How am I going to make it? But I've found the answer: I'm surrounded by loving friends who are there buoying me, supporting me, bringing me vegan donuts and telling me very clearly that it will all be okay. My friends are the comfort food of my life, and they help me get through the day. I hope I do the same for them.

You come into this world alone and die alone, but there's a really long stretch in the middle that can be extraordinarily meaningful and even fun with the right people. And when it's not fun, they'll be with you, too.

Violet and I are getting ready for Barbara's going-away party. Violet insists that all parties have themes. While I came up with "abandonment" and "betrayal," she talked me into the Beatles song "A Little Help from My Friends." She's learning to perform it now and she wants me to sing with her. I told her that I can't do harmony. "Don't worry, Mom," she said, patting my hand, "Barbara can teach you."

ACKNOWLEDGMENTS

Each morning I thank the maker for my own holy trinity/Tony Orlando and Dawn.

Esther Newberg: You save the day several times a week for me, and I love you.

Geoff Kloske: When I was a kid in school playing author/publisher, you were just the fellow I imagined. (A kind man who never used an exclamation point.)

Megan Lynch: Oh, Megan, let's just say if you die (IF), I'm coming with you, because I couldn't manage without you.

Endless thanks to all of my friends at Riverhead Books, especially Jynne Martin, Kate Stark, Marilyn Ducksworth, Mih-Ho Cha, Claire McGinnis, Lydia Hirt, Ali Cardia, Rick Pascocello; and at ICM, especially Kari Stuart and Lyndsey Hemphill.

Love and thanks to the friends I keep: Barbara Warnke, Jancee Dunn, Ann Leary, Patty Marx, Laura Zigman, Claudia Glaser-Mussen, Emma Straub, Vesna Jovanovic,

239

Abigail Gampel, Robin Bahr, Adam Resnick, Rebecca Litchfield, Leslie Verbitsky, Wendy Hammond, Tim Hutton, Judith Newman, Vick Mickunas, Susan Roxborough, John Searles, Martha Broderick, Stoopher & Boots, Lisa Adams, John Sellers, Brenda Copeland, Bethanne Patrick, Lizzie Skurnick, Jenny Maxwell, Megan Gliebe, Karen Keating, Mae Martin, Deb Kogan, Kristin Moavenian, Amy Harmon, Molly Jong-Fast, Gigi Levangie Grazer, Caitlin Abramovitz McNiff, Evelyn Smith, Lauren Gilbert, Tammy Wilson.

Much love and gratitude to my family: Mom, Dad, Matt, Brian, Cheryl, Lara, Mattie, Paul, Violet, and those dogs.

ABOUT THE AUTHOR

Julie Klam grew up in Bedford, New York. She has written for such publications as *O: The Oprah Magazine, Rolling Stone, Harper's Bazaar, Glamour,* and *The New York Times Magazine* and for the VH1 television show *Pop-Up Video,* where she earned an Emmy nomination. She lives in New York City.